"Jared does a great job, with his humorous yet serious style, reminding us of God's perfection in t[...] [...]tencies, fears, and falls—in other words he h[...] [...]p.' Whether you feel you're barely [...]y-saturated obedience, the grace [...]ur-age and remind the saint that [...]nd that perfection is enough for a[...] w[...] [...]s."

Matt Chandler, lead teaching pastor, The Vill[...] [...]urch

"Even though St. Paul wrote that the gospel was 'of first importance,' for some reason most people, even Christians (no less), don't really believe it. What we want are practical steps about how to build a discipleship group and facilitate communication, and though those things aren't wrong in themselves, we want to do it detached from the gospel itself. Which, of course, means that it's doomed to failure before we even start. But this book is different. Jared ties everything he has to say about being and loving disciples to the realities of what Jesus has already done. And that, dear friends, is what sets this wonderful book apart from all the others. Please do buy it. Buy one for a friend. And then read it together—and rejoice in the gospel."

Elyse M. Fitzpatrick, counselor and speaker;
author of *Because He Loves Me*

"Too often discipleship is described in strings of clichés. In *Imperfect Disciple*, Jared Wilson cuts the string, shares his story, and helps readers envision following Jesus in clear, inviting, and realistic ways. It's personal, prophetic, and pastoral and it will help readers reimagine discipleship as a real possibility in the midst of ordinary life."

Mike Cosper, founder and director, Harbor Media

"Wilson takes our idea of discipleship—you know, the list of things we need to do to be a perfectly obedient Christian—and turns it on its head. Discipleship is not about our to-do lists; it's about the glorious gospel. Wilson makes us dizzy with gospel truth and disoriented by beholding the Lamb of God. He helps us refocus so that our obedience is no longer about us. You'll be encouraged as you read *this* book about discipleship."

Trillia Newbell, author of *Enjoy*, *Fear and Faith*, and *United*

"Drawing from Jared Wilson's own story, *The Imperfect Disciple* is a book about grace for people who know about grace. It replaces our neat and tidy notions of discipleship with the real-life messiness of real people—even the "good" ones. For anyone who draws confidence—or shame—from the belief that God is keeping track of their goodness, this book is for you."

Sharon Hodde Miller, writer and speaker

"Follow Jared as he demystifies discipleship on this unpredictable quest into the kindness of Christ."

Christian George, curator of The Spurgeon Library;
assistant professor of historical theology at Midwestern
Seminary; author of *Sex, Sushi, and Salvation*

"While most every Christian would joyfully acknowledge that we are *saved* by grace alone, many of us live as if our ongoing growth in Jesus is not driven and sustained by that same grace. In terms of our discipleship, we suffer from the same self-justifying tendencies that would keep us from the cross to begin with. I'm grateful, then, for this refreshing, grace-saturated, and realistic treatment of what it means to follow Jesus."

Michael Kelley, director of discipleship at Lifeway
Christian Resources; author of *Boring: Finding
an Extraordinary God in an Ordinary Life*

"This is the most refreshing and encouraging book of discipleship I've read in the past decade. For twenty-one years, I had the priceless experience of being pursued, loved, and fathered by a 5'6" gospel Yoda named Jack Miller, who taught me, showed me, and prayed into my bones that my need for Jesus is far greater than I'll realize in this life, but that the grace of Jesus is exponentially more extravagant, outrageous, and liberating than I could ever imagine or hope. With tears, I write this 'blurb,' because Jared has given fresh words, voice, and understanding to this grand reality. Everything about me is imperfect, so I'm just like you. Together, let's seek to discover the much-more-ness of the perfect gospel. Jared helps us do so, with his words and heart."

Scotty Smith, teacher in residence, West End
Community Church, Nashville, Tennessee

"I've read too many 'discipleship' books that made me feel, somehow, less. This book is the exact, wonderful opposite. It's like talking with a very insightful friend about Jesus. It's honest, thoughtful, and unpretentious. Thank you, Jared."

Brant Hansen, storyteller/radio guy, CURE International

"In a world—and church—infatuated with 'leaders,' 'platforms,' and 'influence,' *The Imperfect Disciple* offers a much-needed antidote to our leadership overdose: following. Jared Wilson reminds us that following Christ is not about *what we do* but about *who we are*. And we need be no more—or no less—than flawed but faithful disciples of the One who has already won all of our battles for us."

Karen Swallow Prior, PhD, author of *Booked* and *Fierce
Convictions—The Extraordinary Life of Hannah More*

THE
IMPERFECT
DISCIPLE

Grace for People Who Can't
Get Their Act Together

JARED C. WILSON

BakerBooks

a division of Baker Publishing Group
Grand Rapids, Michigan

© 2017 by Jared C. Wilson

Published by Baker Books
a division of Baker Publishing Group
P.O. Box 6287, Grand Rapids, MI 49516-6287
www.bakerbooks.com

Printed in the United States of America

Library of Congress Cataloging-in-Publication Data
Names: Wilson, Jared C., 1975– author.
Title: The imperfect disciple : grace for people who can't get their act together / Jared C. Wilson.
Description: Grand Rapids : Baker Books, 2017. | Includes bibliographical references.
Identifiers: LCCN 2016052132 | ISBN 9780801018954 (pbk.)
Subjects: LCSH: Grace (Theology)
Classification: LCC BT761.3 .W55 2017 | DDC 248.4—dc23
LC record available at https://lccn.loc.gov/2016052132

Unless otherwise indicated, Scripture quotations are from The Holy Bible, English Standard Version® (ESV®), copyright © 2001 by Crossway, a publishing ministry of Good News Publishers. Used by permission. All rights reserved. ESV Text Edition: 2011

Scripture quotations labeled KJV are from the King James Version of the Bible.

Scripture quotations labeled NIV are from the Holy Bible, New International Version®. NIV®. Copyright © 1973, 1978, 1984, 2011 by Biblica, Inc.™ Used by permission of Zondervan. All rights reserved worldwide. www.zondervan.com

17 18 19 20 21 22 23   8 7 6 5 4

In keeping with biblical principles of creation stewardship, Baker Publishing Group advocates the responsible use of our natural resources. As a member of the Green Press Initiative, our company uses recycled paper when possible. The text paper of this book is composed in part of post-consumer waste.

For Mom and Dad,
who imperfectly but consistently
lived out in front of us
normal, regular, non-weird Christianity.

But she came and knelt before him, saying, "Lord, help me." And he answered, "It is not right to take the children's bread and throw it to the dogs." She said, "Yes, Lord, yet even the dogs eat the crumbs that fall from their masters' table."

Matthew 15:25–27

Contents

Contents

You Should Probably Read This Introduction

(When You Wonder If This Book Is Worth Reading)

Here's a question I used to ask the people I taught in church: "What comes to mind when you hear the word *discipleship*?"

Some people would play word-association and I'd get a string of adjectives in response: *difficult, trusting, adventurous, obedient,* and so forth.

I don't recall many people thinking too long about the question. Very quickly somebody would offer up the "right answer"—at least, the right answer for our context—"Discipleship means following Jesus."

Well, yeah.

Christian discipleship does mean following Jesus. It means following Jesus wherever he goes. It means lashing ourselves to him like a sailor in a storm-tossed boat might lash himself to the mast.

11

When church people say, "Discipleship means following Jesus," I think they tend to picture a group of suntanned dudes in cantata-quality robe costumes peacefully strolling through green pastures, perhaps stopping here and there under the comfortable shade of a tree to watch Jesus smile at them and tousle the hair of precocious children scampering about at his Birkenstocked feet.

Or maybe I'm just cynical.

When I ask, "What comes to mind when you hear the word *discipleship*?" I'd love to hear people answer more along these lines:

"Believing God has a plan for me even when I'm afraid he doesn't."

"Believing God loves me even when I feel like nobody else does."

"Trusting that God is doing something for my good even though my life has always been terrible up till now."

"Following Jesus even though my feelings speak more loudly."

"Denying myself in order to do what's right although I don't really want to."

"Imagining a time when I won't hurt as much as I do now."

"Imagining a time when my spouse or child won't hurt as much as they do now."

You get the idea, I hope. None of those responses really suffices as a definition of *discipleship* like you'd find in a theological dictionary, but they all put more skin on the word, I think.

Sometimes I read books and articles on discipleship and I wonder who in the world they're written for. And then I remember: *Oh, yeah—for people who give the Sunday-school answers in Sunday school but save the real, life-or-death, grasping-for-meaning, gasping-for-breath grappling with God for those rare moments when they're all alone, undistracted, and unable to fend off the crushing sense of their own inadequacies and apprehensions about the world and their place in it.* I tend to think that a lot of the ways the evangelical church teaches discipleship seem designed for people who don't appear to really need it. It's like the übertoned CrossFit junkie who adds a spin class to his weekly schedule, because, well, why not?

I wonder sometimes how all of our steps, tips, and quasi-spiritual "life hacks" come across to the Christian woman who is married to an unbelieving husband completely apathetic to the things of God, to the young Christian whose parents aren't saved and hate that he is, to the husband whose wife seems more interested in Pinterest than in him, to the working-class guys and gals who see through the slick pick-me-ups of the privileged, to the frequently discouraged, the constantly disappointed, and the perennially depressed.

For those of us who have struggled our whole life to get our act together, what does a discipleship built around getting your act together eventually do?

Well, I don't know about you, but it about made me give up.

My gracious publisher, Baker, wanted me to write a book on discipleship. I said, "Okay. But I have one condition: it has to be printed with my blood."

Naturally, they had some health concerns about that—for me and for you. So I clarified. See, I don't want to write the kind of discipleship book most people are too afraid to say they're sick of. I don't want to write a discipleship book for people who put notches on their Belts of Truth every time they read a discipleship book. I don't want to write about being extreme or radical or taking it to the limit or maxing out your potential or reaching the stars or drinking cloud-juice or whatever.

I want to write a discipleship book for normal people, for people like me who know that discipleship means following Jesus—and we know that following Jesus is totally worth it, because Jesus is the end-all, be-all—but we often find that following Jesus takes us to some pretty difficult places.

I want to write a book for the Christians whose discipleship has gotten them a little bloody.

So I said, "How about a book on discipleship for people who don't feel saved each morning until they've had at least two cups of coffee? How about a book on following Jesus for the guy or gal sitting there in small group always wondering if it's safe to say what they're thinking? For the sake of the cut-ups and the screwups, the tired and the torn-up, the weary and the wounded—how about we demystify discipleship?"

And they said, astonishingly, "Okay."

So here you have it, in your cold little hands. This book on following Jesus is for all of you people who, like me, are tired of the mass-marketed, self-helpy "be a better Christian" projects. It's not printed with my blood, but I did bleed on the pages a little bit.

1

Sin and the Art of Soul Maintenance

(When You Can't Get Your Act Together)

In short, I am a riddle to myself;
a heap of inconsistence.

John Newton[1]

My gospel is a little sweaty and ragged around the edges. The print is smeared a little bit, and it's flat and conformed to the contour of my upper thigh from hiding in my front pocket. Maybe your gospel looks like mine. Sometimes it can feel weird to show it to somebody.

When I was in the ninth grade I lived in Albuquerque, New Mexico, and every day during that freshman year I walked home from school with my friend Steve. We had to walk a long way from El Dorado High School along Juan Tabo Boulevard before reaching the turnoff to our neighborhood. Steve was short and round; I was tall and skinny. We looked like a teenage Abbot and Costello ambling down the sidewalk. We were the frequent victims of drive-by shouting. We'd laugh about it, usually, because it was often difficult to make out the substance of this verbal abuse, thanks to the Doppler effect and the generally loud traffic noise on the street. But mainly I recall our sexuality being questioned.

One day, somebody threw a Ziploc baggie of water at us. Not a water balloon. A Ziploc baggie full of water. Steve got hit in the back. He was a pretty good sport about it, honestly. After it—splat!—smacked him square between the shoulder blades, it plopped unbroken onto the sidewalk. We stared at it for a few seconds. A baggie of water? Who *does* that?

Whenever we made it to the turnoff into the neighborhood, we had about fifteen more minutes of walking before we split off for our respective homes. Once we'd cleared the *American Ninja Warrior* course of Juan Tabo, those fifteen minutes were really the only uninterrupted time of talking we had on our journey home. We usually spent them talking about Arnold Schwarzenegger movies or rap music. I usually also spent them trying to figure out how to talk to Steve about Jesus.

I kept this tract in my pocket. And every day I thought about how to bring it out and explain its contents to Steve. But there never seemed to be an ideal opening in the conversation. You can't talk about *Predator* and *The Running Man* and somehow smoothly transition into the Romans Road. Still more difficult is this transition from Steve waxing enthusiastic about "The Humpty Dance." I mean, I wanted to, but I couldn't figure out how to get from being called "fags" by some stupid meat-head with his stupid meat-head face hanging out the window of his stupid meat-head El Camino, or having a baggie of water thrown at us, to God having a wonderful plan for Steve's life.

So the tract stayed put, for months on end.

Let me back up a bit. Because to understand my anxiety and apprehension about evangelizing the bejeezus out of Steve on these walks home, you have to understand how I'd been trained to evangelize—how I'd been *discipled*.

I grew up in the eighties attending a relatively normal Baptist church. The church was neither very traditional nor very modern. It was your run-of-the-mill, slacks-on-Sunday-morning and jeans-on-Sunday-night evangelical congregation. The gospel of Jesus was there and every sinner heard it—every sinner, that is, except those who'd already heard it. The idea that grace was for Christians too was somewhat of a foreign concept; grace was Christianity 101. Once you had God's grace, you had to move on to bigger things, to what we called "deeper" things, things like charts of the end-times and pledging abstinence until marriage. (I really hoped I'd be able to get married and have sex before Jesus returned, which might tell you a little something about how poorly we'd been pitched the concept of Christ's glorious second coming.)

Grace got me into God's family. I walked an aisle when I was five or six, was quickly baptized thereafter, said the sinner's prayer a second time when I was twelve just for good measure, and was rebaptized at fifteen to make extra sure. I had that grace in my pocket, sure enough. But it was pretty clear that now I was sort of hanging on by a thread. And as a neurotic, sinful, messed-up kid, I felt like I was constantly dangling over hellfire.

There were endless checklists and progress charts tracking my growth in the Christian life. By the time I got to junior high school, I was committed to looking like the best

Christian kid I could be. This is a hard place to be if you're not exactly sure Jesus loves you, or even *likes* you. I kind of felt like I was a Christian only because the Bible says "God is love," and so if I signed on the dotted line, he *had* to take me. I was exploiting his own loophole.

By the time I reached the ninth grade, I had already sensed a calling into vocational ministry, which only intensified my commitment to playing the part of a good religious kid. And this is what made ninth-grade Sunday school so excruciating. Every Sunday morning, at the start of class, our teacher would ask us who we'd witnessed to the previous week. Most of us, I'm convinced, just made up our evangelistic encounters. Brave souls would say "nobody" and offer some kind of excuse. But the bottom line was if you weren't witnessing, you probably weren't even saved yourself.

At the time, I had no framework for "witnessing" beyond the evangelistic sales pitch we'd all been encouraged to engage in since childhood, the same kind of sales pitch that roped us into the faith ourselves. "Witnessing" wasn't really about bearing witness to others about the grace of God in your life; it wasn't even about telling somebody the good news, really. It was about getting somebody to admit they were a sinner and then somehow getting them to pray a formulaic prayer. I like to call this "closing the deal."

My Sunday school teacher was like the *Glengarry Glen Ross* of evangelism, and we were to Always. Be. Closing.

Well, I'm sorry, but I was a terrible closer. Heck, I was a terrible *opener*.

I dreaded going to Sunday school and not being able to answer for why I hadn't witnessed to anybody and why I was a terrible Christian who deserved to live in the cruddy "We

Had to Let Them in Here Because They Prayed the Sinner's Prayer" section of heaven for all eternity.

I grew weary from the good works I wasn't doing.

Finally, one Friday on our walk home from school, after Steve and I made the turnoff from Juan Tabo into our neighborhood, I spent the ensuing fifteen minutes working up the courage to witness to him. Then, when it came time for us to part ways, I reached into my pocket, pulled out that damp little gospel, and held it out to him. I quickly said, "Hey, will you read this? I have to say at church that I gave it to somebody, so just take it and say you read it. But you don't really have to if you don't want to."

Truly the most compelling invitation to repent and follow Jesus ever delivered.

Steve looked at the thin little tract in my hand. He just sort of shrugged, said "Okay," and took it.

I had staved off damnation for at least one more week.

What's Wrong with Me?

I don't know how to explain my primary personal malfunction except to say that there is constantly a shadow of guilt overlaying my thoughts. I want to take you back to the time I was first baptized, back in that plain vanilla Baptist church when I was five or six years old. I don't remember much about the experience at all. I don't remember what I was wearing. I don't remember anything that was said. I don't remember going down into the water. I don't remember coming up. I don't remember if people clapped or if my mom hugged me afterward. I don't remember much about it at all. Except! I do remember the moment right before the baptism—quite vividly, in fact.

I was waiting my turn to the right of the baptistery, which was elevated on the front wall of the sanctuary, situated centrally above the choir loft. I was standing on the bare plywood floor that led up to the baptismal steps, behind a wall and out of sight of the congregation, waiting to be invited into the pool. The church was singing whatever hymn preceded the baptisms that day. I don't remember what hymn it was, but I remember the sound of the organ. It was loud and ominous, shaking the thin wooden floor. The walls seemed to vibrate with every note played. The vengeful Spirit of God himself was the wind through those bellows, and I could feel him blowing across my hollow bones to make that thunderous bottle music. I was scared.

That's what I remember thirty-five years later.

In a lot of ways, I have felt haunted by those gale-force tones all my life. And when it comes to my spiritual state, I very often still feel like that little boy—hidden, small, and trembling, waiting on a welcome to come get clean, and finally getting clean by the skin of my teeth.

My "reconversion" at twelve years of age was not much different in tone. We were still attending the same church, having returned to my hometown after a few years away, and somebody decided it'd be a great idea to show those "left behind" movies. Now, I don't mean the recent Kirk Cameron *Left Behind* movies, the terrible ones adapted from those terrible novels. I'm talking about the 1970s Larry Norman–crooning "You've been left beeee-hind" movies, the ones with dudes and dudettes running around in striped kneesocks trying to escape the antichrist's UN (or whatever it was). I'm not sure what exactly was going on in those movies except that the rapture happened and people got left behind, including people who claimed to be Christians. And in the end, if you decided to take your second chance and *really* get saved this time, you got your head chopped off. The story lines were a little difficult to follow unless you spent your life neck-deep in dispensational premillennialism, but they were honest-to-God frightening to timid souls like my own.

I started having nightmares. I know evangelicals like to joke about discovering nobody's in the house and suspecting "rapture," but this legitimately happened to me a few times. I'd wake up in the middle of the night and check my parents' bedroom to make sure they were still there. I spent a few nights sleeping on their bedroom floor.

Eventually I prayed "the prayer" a second time. Then that second baptism. Wash, rinse, repeat. You could say that I very effectively had the hell scared out of me.

I think back on all of this and the kind of discipleship that came along with it, and honestly it's a wonder I'm not cowering in a corner as I type this very paragraph. But do you know what? It would be a huge mistake to assume that everything that's wrong with me as it pertains to my spiritual temperament and religious sensibilities is the fault of my church upbringing. I know plenty of friends and family raised in this same environment, or church cultures very similar to it, who are just fine and dandy right now. They're confident, self-assured, highly functional, perfectly happy people. (Those jerks.)

But seriously. A lot of what ails me was obviously not helped by the tenor of my adolescent discipleship, but the blame really lies deep inside myself. I was born a spiritually dysfunctional person. I grew up kind of neurotic and fearful, but my biggest problem isn't anything anybody or any place did to me.

I think of the story (more than likely apocryphal) wherein G. K. Chesterton responded to an article in the *London Times* titled, "What's Wrong with the World?" Apparently, Chesterton did not agree with their conclusions, because he allegedly wrote a letter to the paper in response:

> *Dear Sir:*
> *Regarding your article "What's Wrong with the World?"*
> *I am.*
>
> *Yours truly,*
> *G. K. Chesterton*

This is all very clever, see, but my man Gilbert Keith got it entirely wrong. He should have written the *London Times* to say, "I'll tell you what's wrong with the world. That imbecile, Jared Wilson." I am confident that if he knew *me*, he would not have so casually suggested himself as the source of all the world's ills.

I have that ominous organ playing inside me. My heart is a haunted house—broken, ramshackle, weathered and boarded-up and filled with the mournful sound of the Hound of Heaven howling through the slats.

I do have my good days, mind you. Quite a lot of them, actually. And most of my days are mixes of good and bad feelings, mostly good. I manage fairly well at keeping it together. I mean, really, I just reread the previous several paragraphs and I guess I should apologize to you for sounding so mopey.

It's just that whenever I actually think about how I'm doing, it doesn't seem as though I'm doing very well at all. In fact, most of the good that I've accomplished in my life and most of the good things that have happened in my life have come nowhere close to fixing what's really going on inside of me.

This is why I resonate with the apostle Paul when he's driving down that Romans Road and decides to turn left on red into Romans chapter 7. I know some scholars argue that Romans 7 is not a description of the Christian life but rather is Paul describing his life before his conversion. Maybe they're right. Or maybe, like Chesterton writing that letter to the *London Times*, they just aren't aware of my existence. Because it sure seems like Paul's got my number. He says, in part:

> For I know that nothing good dwells in me, that is, in my flesh. For I have the desire to do what is right, but not the ability to carry it out. For I do not do the good I want, but the evil I do not want is what I keep on doing. Now if I do what I do not want, it is no longer I who do it, but sin that dwells within me.
>
> So I find it to be a law that when I want to do right, evil lies close at hand. For I delight in the law of God, in my inner being, but I see in my members another law waging war against the law of my mind and making me captive to the law of sin that dwells in my members. (Rom. 7:18–23)

My Bible has assigned a subheading to this section of Romans that reads "The Law and Sin." I would like to modestly propose the editors change that heading to read "Why We Can't Get Our Act Together."

Paul is careening back and forth between right and wrong, good and bad, holy and unholy. He knows the difference. This is one indication, although a minor one, that he may be speaking to his post-conversion life, as he has elsewhere said that the unsaved don't even understand the things of God (1 Cor. 2:14) and that the unrighteous aren't wrestling with the truth but *suppressing* it (Rom. 1:18).

Secondly, however, he also indicates that he delights in the law in his inner being (7:22), which is a strange thing to say if he's referring to being lost, even to being a lost "Jew among Jews," since the biblical indictment of self-righteousness is demonstrably that it only delights in the law *behaviorally*—that its "inner being" is, as Jesus says, rotting and dead (Matt. 23:27).

Nevertheless, whether Paul is discussing pre-conversion or post-conversion struggle, I read Romans 7 and think, *Man, Paul, you get me—you really get me.* He's got me nailed here. The good stuff I want to do? I find myself, on the regular, unable (really, unwilling) to do it. The bad stuff I know not to do? I find myself, *tout de suite*, all up in that.

Here's a plainer way to put it: I do things that I know are bad and I avoid doing things that I know are good. This makes me imminently unqualified to write one of those awesome, take-the-next-hill, "be the change you want to see in the world" books on discipleship churned out ever-presently by the evangelical leadership-industrial complex.

But on the other hand, it makes me uniquely and distinctly qualified for the hope Paul offers in response to the crushing predicament bemoaned by Romans 7.

It turns out—and you need to read this closely, so I hereby advise you to actually pull this book closer to your face and get the following words right in front of your milky little corneas . . . well, not that close; you look like a weirdo.

Hold it up. Read it close. Drink it deep.

It turns out, actually, that—*get this*—Jesus is looking specifically for the people who can't get their act together.

I know, right? I swear I am not making this up!

Paul's sense of hopeless exasperation reaches a crescendo in verse 24: "Wretched man that I am! Who will deliver me from this body of death?" He feels caught, trapped, like the corpse of his old life is still hanging on to his ankle and he can't move on. He's tried pulling himself up by his bootstraps but he got them tangled around his neck and now he's choking to death.

This is exactly the kind of self-despair Jesus is listening for.

"Thanks be to God through Jesus Christ our Lord!" Paul says in verse 25, and you can almost hear him panting like a guy just pulled out of the water from drowning.

Every day, I wake up into Romans 7. Every dadgum day. My alarm goes off and I sit up in bed, my uncoffeed consciousness groggily gearing up for sins—both of omission and of commission. I'm engaged in the flesh before I even get my feet on the carpet.

And yet, right there beside me, laid out like the day's outfit for school, are new mercies. Romans 8 lies right there, spooning Romans 7 in a full-size bed, no wiggle room.

There is therefore now no condemnation for those who are in Christ Jesus. For the law of the Spirit of life has set you free in Christ Jesus from the law of sin and death. For God has done what the law, weakened by the flesh, could not do. (Rom. 8:1–3)

How do we get out of this mess? We can't. But God does what we cannot do. So while the storm of Romans 7 rages inside of us, the truth of Romans 8 has us safe and sound. Within the spiritual ecosystem of God's saving sovereignty, in fact, our struggle is like the little squall stirred up in a snow globe.

God is collecting all these little storms. He is doing something beautiful with us and even *in* us and *through* us. This is the great light that overcomes the shadow world of Romans 7. It is the good news for all of us who can't get our act together. We are exactly the kind of people God is looking for. We are exactly the kind of people God is using. We are exactly the kind of people God loves.

What's Wrong with You?

Every day you drift naturally into Romans 7. You don't need any help with that. It's just that your wheels are naturally out of alignment. You're just wobbly, okay? You're going to get where you want to go eventually. So here's what you do.

As early in the day and as often as you can, you turn on the light of Romans 8. You bring Romans 8 into Romans 7 and you say, "Look what I found, everybody!" You're the gal who's brought your fiancé home to meet the family, and it turns out he's a much better catch than anybody, including yourself, ever thought you'd end up with. He's a rich doctor-slash-fighter pilot who spends his summers digging wells for orphans in the Congo or something, okay? And Aunt Bitterness is sitting over there in the corner of the living room stewing away, ready to take you on a trip down angry memory lane, and you're like, "Aunt Bitterness, I'd like you to meet my fiancé, Dr. Gospel. Isn't he dreamy?" And there's Uncle Lazy sitting at the table medicating his feelings with three Egg McMuffins, and you bring Dr. Gospel over, and Uncle Lazy instantly perks up and realizes how embarrassing he looks in the face of such accomplishment. And there's your twin sister Pride sitting there in the middle of the room, like she owns the place, but when Dr. Gospel walks up to her, she gets up and offers him her seat without a word.

It's a little like that. You introduce the truth of Romans 8 to every corner of the room, every dark place in your heart, as often as you can, as much as you can, as fiercely as you can.

Every day. It has to happen every day. Because what's wrong with you and me is that we're still on this side of glory, and so long as we're on this side of glory, there will always be more sanctifying to go through. I've met some people who think they're all good-and-sanctified already, and I like to tenderly suggest to them that they have much further to go than they realize.

When we die or the Lord returns, whichever comes first, we will be instantly glorified—made like him, like *whoosh*, in the blink of an eye—but until that moment, we're trekking across Romans 7 in a three-legged race with our pride through thigh-deep mud. But Romans 8 turns the boosters on. Romans 8 is like walking on water.

And I don't mean you've got to literally be only drawing from Romans 8. I just mean that the problem Romans 7 highlights—which is echoed throughout the Bible—can only be overcome with the antidote Romans 8 presents—which reverberates throughout the Bible as well.

But this is where Romans 7 and 8 as representatives are quite helpful. They help us diagnose our real dysfunctions.

We are constantly told that our problems are primarily about self-actualization, about success or happiness or just acting right or feeling right. And we definitely have problems with all of these things, but they are not our main problems.

I think, deep down, you probably know this. It's the reason why, try as you might to address all these issues, you never feel quite *fixed*.

Discipleship as Soul Maintenance

You and I need tuning up in the gospel every day.

This is how I like to think about discipleship, then—not just following Jesus, but *refollowing* Jesus every day. We go off track so easily.

When I was pastoring, I much admired the dominant biblical portrait of the pastorate—a shepherd with his flock. But any seasoned ministry veteran will tell you that pastoral ministry is very often less like herding sheep and more like herding cats. The prophet Isaiah says that "all we like sheep have gone astray" (53:6), and I wonder if it's because he wasn't around cats very much. Sheep tend to go astray because they are dumbly distracted. That's a little like us. But cats go astray because they are smug investors in their own narcissistic autonomy. That's a lot like us.

Then you put us on this confusing, twisty journey called life, and there's just so much that can go wrong. It especially goes wrong when we aren't clear on exactly what's wrong. Do you know why there are a thousand fresh self-help books every year? It's because they don't work. We keep looking for the answer within us, as if we'll find it in the same place as the problems. Self-help is like sticking your broken hand in the blender, thinking that'll fix it.

Our souls are greatly troubled. They are greatly troubled especially when we don't feel they are. Sin is deceptive. The devil comes as an angel of light. The way to destruction is wide and easygoing. All of this spells trouble for the one who doesn't work at deciphering the riddle of himself.

Our souls need a good looking at. Most people don't and won't do this. In fact, all day our souls are whispering to us that they need some tending, but we're listening to the noise of social media or satellite television or pop religion, making sure the squeaky wheel gets drowned out.

What we need to do is roll up our sleeves, lift up the hood, and take a look at our inner selves. We need to get the instructions out, get our hands on some tools. The soul is a tricky thing, and needy. We have to feed it well, keep it well-nourished and well-lubricated. We have to speak to it rightly, like the psalmist—"Hey, soul, what's going on with you? Why are you messed up today?"[2]

We see the tendency to self-worship, the tendency to stray from God's will and to rebel against his good orders, and like an enlightened mechanic we say, "There's your problem, right there."

The diagnosis is helpful. If we don't diagnose the problem correctly, we cannot address it effectively. We see that our soul is prone to slipping out of gear, dropping quite easily and quickly from Romans 8 to Romans 7. So here we go again, bringing Romans 8 to bear on ourselves.

Some of us like to call this work "preaching the gospel to ourselves."

Look at what that songwriter is doing in Psalm 42. He's preaching to himself. But it's not advice that he's preaching.

He knows throwing good advice into the darkness of the soul is like throwing popcorn into outer space.

No, he doesn't need good advice; he needs good news. Wouldn't you rather have the antidote for sin than an eight-step treatment plan to simply medicate against it? The psalmist sings:

> By day the LORD commands his steadfast love,
>   and at night his song is with me,
>   a prayer to the God of my life. (42:8)

In the end, as in the beginning, it is not our good intentions or even our good deeds that will get us out of the muck of ourselves. It is God's rescuing hand. It is his enduring announcement over us messed-up creatures, "I love you," that changes everything.

Now, some Christians don't think this way. It seems too easy. But if it really were easy, more people would do it. No, it's very difficult because it means, essentially, admitting *we don't have what it takes.*

I take a look at my messed-up soul every day. I feel completely overwhelmed and underequipped. And so I hold on to the gospel. I pour some gospel into my soul. I am good to go another day. I might be crawling through that day or I might be balled up in my bed, unwilling to charge the Valley of Elah that is my life, but the smile of God is over me continually. Day and night his steadfast love sustains me.

By God's grace, then, disciples of Jesus look for the places we have yet to surrender to him, the places where we've given up ground, the tender spots we want to hide, the stubborn spaces we want to protect, and we ask him humbly to help us. He will never say no to that. Bit by bit, day by day, turning and returning, we reorient the engine of our life around Jesus. The problem is the same every day but the mercies are new, and the disciples of Jesus will plunder them with abandon. He *wants* us to!

You've got to maintain your soul this way or you will not maintain it at all. You've got to hook your soul on this anchor called Christ or you will lose it, I assure you.

The soul is a complicated thing. The soul is a wormhole, multidimensional, polyhedral. We have outer space inside of us. And we think we can *manage* this? Give this thing a religious pep talk here and there?

No, we can only hope to maintain these souls somehow, tend to them, send out into ourselves the radio signal of the deep magic of the gospel. It's a great comfort to know that the announcement of the finished work of Christ is specifically designed for this inner-spatial mission.

I don't know how my high-school friend Steve is doing these days. I wish I did. I've tried to look him up on Facebook, and he's either not there or he's changed so much I don't recognize him. But if I could get one more chance, I'd love to take a little walk with him down Juan Tabo Boulevard. After a few decades of living, I imagine we'd both agree that life is kind of a mix of *The Running Man* and getting baggies of warm water thrown at your back. But I wouldn't struggle so much to tell him about the hope I've found. Because I've actually found hope in that little message I used to feel nervous about. Now it's *me* I feel nervous about. The only thing I feel confident in is that message!

My soul is not much to look at but it is safeguarded by the One who paid himself for me. This is really the only hope we've got. Sin is our problem. Jesus is the answer. There's no two ways about it. And if you're not too good for him, you can have him. It helps especially if you're bad.

Look, my gospel is a little sweaty and ragged around the edges. But it will still be in my pocket, worn from good use and serious study—print smudged from the grip of desperate belief—when Christ comes gently crashing back into earth to ask me about it. When the proverbial roll is called up yonder, I'll be there, if this gospel has anything to say about it.

2 Good News for Losers

(When You Don't See the Advantage of Being at the Bottom)

She said, "Yes, Lord, yet even the dogs
eat the crumbs that fall
from their masters' table."

Matthew 15:27

My gospel is well worn. Its pages are thin from use. I've run over it and over it—by myself and with others, and for whatever reason, it doesn't seem to wear completely out. It feels like cloth now, delicate and soft. I dare not replace it, though, because it's the only one I've got.

I bring this gospel out when I'm discipling others.

Okay, wait. *Discipling* is not a word we find in the Scriptures. Nor do we find *discipleship*, for that matter. Let me start over.

I bring this soft-as-cloth gospel out of my pocket when I am *helping others follow Jesus*. Sometimes we are in an office.

Many times we are in a coffee shop or restaurant. Oftentimes we are in their home or mine. Too many times we are in the dark cave of their shame, crowded out by the stalagmites formed from a thousand years of sin, and we're holding that gospel up to every narrow beam of light we can find.

Sometimes the pages of the gospel are hard to read in those circumstances, so we just use it to wipe our brow or dry our tears.

The sins of garden-variety human beings are frustratingly redundant. I don't recall ever moving on from one area of battle to another with anybody I've ever "done discipleship" with. Nobody ever "achieved victory." It's the same old thing every time. We like our ruts, and our ruts like us.

And it's not just the sins that don't seem to go away; it's the wounds too. These two things are not the same! We have to get that straight, first of all. Too many foolish teachers in the church equate wounds with sins, and vice versa, and this needlessly frustrates people's following of Jesus. We further traumatize victims when we tell them their wounds are sins, and we demotivate repenters when we tell them their sins are wounds.

But this confusion is somewhat understandable in that both sins and wounds linger. Our deepest wounds and our deepest sins are both awfully persistent.

Too many times to count, I'd be sitting with some wounded person recounting their past week, a mix of good times and bad, but the culmination of which has led them back to my counsel, hungry for a good report, eager for some final, concluding release. I recall one of my favorite disciples, an early-middle-aged woman who was a relatively new believer. She loved the things of God and was thirsty for the living

water of the gospel. But she still struggled with angry out-
bursts (sins) and she still suffered from the trauma of abuse
as a child (wounds). These were very much connected realities in her soul, and every time we met we would spend our
time working through the routine maintenance of grace,
untangling sins from wounds, sorting out her responsibilities
from her vulnerabilities, distinguishing what she owed from
what was owed to her.

Every time we met she asked the same questions:

How do I forget what happened to me?

How do I forgive the people who hurt me?

How do I control my temper?

Is it okay if I'm angry with God?

Does God stop loving me when I'm angry with him?

What if I never get better?

To tire of this routine was natural. She was tired of living the life, feeling the pain, battling the sin that made this
routine necessary! But every time we'd rehearse the gospel
again, clinging with furtive fingers to that well-worn message.

In and out, they'd come. In and out, I'd come. Men and
women, singles and married, young and old. Too hurt to
talk or too hurt to stay silent. We ran down a lifetime of sin
and pain in our little discipleship spaces.

And then sometimes—*lots* of times—all I could do was
share that gospel. The darkness would drift over us, the
pain too heavy, the grief too fresh, like this person was
sending out shock waves, radiating some kind of spiritual

EMP shorting out all our circuits. We'd end up sitting *shiva*, saying nothing, simply mourning the reality that we were back here again, facing the same deals and devils. Sometimes I'd think of things to say, but if I was wise that day I wouldn't say them.

Plenty of times, though, if it weren't for that gospel, I simply wouldn't have words at all. This happened a lot. And I could feel their judgment, their own silent desperation tugging at my heart, their eyes pleading with me to say something, anything, that would make it better, make it different, make it go away. I heard them in my head: *You're the religious professional, for God's sake! You're the expert, aren't you? You're the one with the Bible! We pay your salary with the tithe money we could've gone on vacation with!*

I feared my silence only contributed to their pain. (*If the pastor doesn't know what to say to fix it, then it can't be fixed.*) I worried that in these times the hardest thing about my disciples' wounds and sins was my not having any words with which to address them.

I found myself frequently saying, "I don't know what to say."

One time I sat in a room in the wake of a broken marriage. I have run this scenario back and forth through my mind countless times. Nobody's perfect, so I could have done better. There's no denying that. But I believe I did what I could. I didn't create their marriage problems. I didn't make him an angry person or make her a sullen one. I didn't make him treat her harshly any more than I made her cheat on him. I wasn't responsible for the relational fault lines between them. I was the shepherd discovering their sins and wounds at least a decade after the devastation had become a grand canyon running through their souls and through their life together. And yet I sat in this room with them, and with God and a few others as witnesses, and listened to this woman say—to me, not to her husband—"You weren't there for me."

She had decided to call it quits after all our counseling sessions, phone calls, check-ins, prayers.

"You weren't there for me."

For the others in the room it just hung there in the air. Nobody swatted it down.

For me, it flooded right into my heart, a blast of cancerous radiation.

I didn't know what to say.

I wanted to defend myself. I wanted to push back, hard. I wanted to argue. But I didn't know if I should. I didn't think it would help.

More had been exposed than my accuser had known. She had triggered the deep sense of inadequacy and disqualification that always lay under the surface of my soul. I don't truly believe I failed her the way she thought I had, but her words ripped my frail assurance apart.

If I could go back in time, I would tell many church folks I pastored that I didn't need any help feeling like a failure. Feeling like a failure is my default state.

And so this woman's words hurt not just in the way they were false but more in the way they were true.

I was pushed again to own my basic nothingness and embrace the One who is everything.

This reminds me of the time Jesus called a woman a dog. It's hard to understate the harshness of those words. It's easy to overstate them, however, and I've heard a few preachers make dumb references to "the b-word," which not only *wouldn't* Jesus have done but culturally speaking *couldn't* have done, since the historical definition of that English word—from the Germanic *bicce*—as "female dog" is as foreign to the Aramaic Jesus spoke as the modern slang appropriation is to the culture in which he spoke it. So no: Jesus wasn't calling that woman the b-word.

But he wasn't exactly being nice either. Jesus was doing what he normally did—provoking a response. And not just for kicks. No, Jesus didn't work that way. He got right to the point, cutting to the quick and penetrating to the heart, not because he got some weird thrill out of making people uncomfortable but because he found it imminently agreeable to air out people's shame that he might cover it for them.

You cannot vanquish what you cannot expose.

We'll come back and revisit this eye-widening episode at the end of the chapter, but for now let's just let it hang there. Let it bug us a little bit. Let it get stuck between a couple of back teeth like a thread of gristle.

Jesus called this woman a dog.

The Sermon on the Mount Is Religious Business as Unusual

Many, many people—including many church people—have this asinine idea that Jesus showed up on earth two thousand years ago and loosened everything up. You know, like everything was so boring and traditional and legalistic or whatever, and then God sent Jesus Christ to "Keep Jerusalem Weird" or something, like he's formed some hippie commune for people with "Coexist" bumper stickers on their cars.

As I mentioned, it's not just the unbelieving world that thinks of Jesus that way; it's a whole lot of people who identify as Christians too.

The problem with this perspective is evident when one actually reads the pages of the Gospels. In these pages we find Jesus equating lust with adultery and hatred with murder, promising to bring a sword instead of peace, commanding people to love those who are trying to kill them, telling a guy to skip his father's funeral, calling men to quit their jobs, and cursing random fig trees. Most people understand that Jesus was shaking things up, but most people assume he was doing so to disrupt those *other* people. (He had a few things to say about that kind of thinking too.)

There is virtually no part of Jesus's life and ministry that isn't vastly misunderstood. We have turned the incarnation into a once-a-year precious moment, the parables into moralistic fables, the miracles into production values. We've managed to somehow turn the message of the cross into one of mere martyrdom (which scandalizes almost nobody) and the reality of the resurrection into a metaphor for turning over a new leaf (which convinces fewer still).

And then you come to the Sermon on the Mount. This is our Lord's *pièce de résistance*, his monumental line in the sand for all humanity. This is the passage of Scripture from which fans of Jesus most often quote. "Don't judge." "Love your enemies." "Turn the other cheek."

All of which they're quoting out of some lame self-interest. They think they're being revolutionary when really they are only backing religious business as usual—using holy words for personal gain.

We are idiots when it comes to the Sermon on the Mount. And, in fact, the Sermon on the Mount makes us idiots. We come up against it and see what it makes of our striving, our ambition, our jockeying for position, and it puts us in our place. But rather than humble ourselves before it we try to co-opt it and spin it, turn it into a set of Christian fortune cookies.

No portion of the Sermon is more ripe for this thievery than the introductory announcement we have traditionally called the Beatitudes. In the Beatitudes, Jesus Christ makes a series of proclamations about the purpose and effect of his kingdom that is breaking into the world.

> And he opened his mouth and taught them, saying:
>> "Blessed are the poor in spirit, for theirs is the kingdom of heaven.
>> "Blessed are those who mourn, for they shall be comforted.
>> "Blessed are the meek, for they shall inherit the earth.
>> "Blessed are those who hunger and thirst for righteousness, for they shall be satisfied.
>> "Blessed are the merciful, for they shall receive mercy.
>> "Blessed are the pure in heart, for they shall see God.
>> "Blessed are the peacemakers, for they shall be called sons of God.
>> "Blessed are those who are persecuted for righteousness' sake, for theirs is the kingdom of heaven.
>> "Blessed are you when others revile you and persecute you and utter all kinds of evil against you falsely on my account." (Matt. 5:2–11)

Blessed, blessed, blessed. What is Jesus doing? He's telling the losers that it's their turn now—or, at least, that it will be soon.

I once read one of those self-helpy quasi-Christian leadership books for type A personalities where the author turned "Blessed are the meek" into law. Instead of being an announcement it became an action point. Being meek is how we get the blessing, he was saying, but in doing so he had to redefine everything else about the Sermon on the Mount, including turning Jesus's promised blessings into success in our project or workplace—basically, anything that Jesus *wasn't* referring to.

This writer also had to assure us stupid readers, as so many who teach on this passage do, that being meek was not about being weak; it's instead about "power under control." You know, because God forbid anybody admit they're weak or deal with weakness or wrestle at all with Paul saying in 2 Corinthians 12 that, strengths be damned, he's going to boast in his weakness.

So set all that aside for a second, and I'll tell you what really bugged me about this part of the book: this writer had done what too many of our disciplers do. He turned gospel into law; he took news and turned it into advice.

Jesus says, "I am bringing a blessing to the meek." This guy is saying, "Become meek and you'll get blessed." It sort of makes sense, and of course the Bible does command us to humble ourselves, but Jesus seems to be speaking to people who are already meek in some way, who've perhaps been *made* meek in some way, by some circumstance or experience. This author was treating meekness as if it's something we might put on, a position we might access to achieve particular results.

This is what troubles me most about the way evangelical leadership culture approaches humility—it always seems like an angle. "Humility" always seems like something we *do* in order to get what we want.

I don't think this is what Jesus has in mind in the Beatitudes.

And I don't think evangelical leadership culture has a very consistent reading of the Beatitudes when it comes to this stuff, because Jesus also says, "Blessed are you who are poor" (Luke 6:20) but very few evangelical leadership gurus I know would advocate intentionally seeking poverty. (Though quite a few Christians I know might.)

No, the Beatitudes are not laws. They aren't steps or tips. These blessings are good tidings! They are announcements of something happening, not instructions of things to do. The Beatitudes are beautiful entailments of the good news of God's kingdom, which has come in and through the person and work of Jesus Christ—that is to say, they do not come in and through the strategies of therapeutic Christian moralizing.

We just don't get the Sermon on the Mount, or Jesus's ministry in general, like his immediate hearers did. Jesus wasn't turning things upside down. He was turning them right side up.

This is why the good news is good news for those at the bottom. Think of every category of person spoken to in the Beatitudes:

The spiritually impoverished.
The emotionally devastated.
The psychologically weak.
The culturally oppressed.

The inwardly pure.

The relationally calm.

The physically abused.

The personally accused.

Culturally speaking, do we cherish these people? Are these the kinds of people we typically feature on magazine covers or in awards shows?

What about Christian culture? Do we buy these people's books by the millions? Do we go to conferences to hear them? Do we podcast them? Do we listen to them on the radio?

No. We're too busy being played by those who've learned to game the system. We don't really care to hear from these people. They're messy, a little weird, socially awkward, kind of needy, and not very put together. What can they teach us? I mean, what can they teach us about what we really want? They aren't winners. We don't want a word from them.

And we don't typically have a word *for* them.

And yet these people are exactly the ones Jesus is speaking to. His words are especially designed for and specifically targeted at . . . well, *losers*.

Reading the Beatitudes as either hyperspiritual law-deliverance or hippie-spiritual law-avoidance are equally adventures in missing the point. The Beatitudes are instead a shot across the bow at worldly and traditional cultural values.

Wait. No.

The Beatitudes are a shot right into the side of these cultural values, a heat-seeking missile into the rusty hull of that worn old battleship, the SS Works Righteousness. They are an alien invasion, a monolith dropped right out of the other dimension like the thing in *2001* that drove all the apes crazy.

Some got smarter, some got meaner, but they all got different because the landscape of reality had been changed. That's what the Beatitudes do. They change reality.

And this cannot be good news for those who are, spiritually speaking, sitting at the head of the conference table. It cannot be good news for those who are, you know, feeling their own way through life by following the positive energy, man. This cannot be good news for those churches whose offices resemble *Glengarry Glen Ross*. This cannot be good news for those clinking wine glasses over burnt steaks while making a deal on the vivisected corpses of babies. It cannot be good news for those trying to game the system.

But isn't it good news for those of us in the caves?

Jesus Wasn't Blowing Smoke

We live in a world that's desperate for the real Jesus. Not some synthetic version of him. The real Jesus and what he really said and really did. The despair is getting thicker in this world. It will not be remedied by the syrupy platitudes that often pass for Christianity.

I read *Between the World and Me* by Ta-Nehisi Coates on a flight from Kansas City to Dallas and landed with my protons rearranged. The book is ostensibly a letter from Coates to his teenage son about what it means to be black in America. The book is profoundly earthy. There is a lot of discussion about the black body, what it means to live inside of it, what it means for a black body to exist in this culture, and what it meant (and still means) that black bodies were kidnapped, enslaved, and tortured. You cannot escape the utter soberness about reality in this book, and that is one of its great strengths—Coates doesn't flinch. In fact, he actually can't. To flinch, to turn away, to ignore is only an option for the privileged. Coates delves into the reality he's been thrust into by the collision between America and his blackness. It's in the depths of reality that he finds—and we find—sentimental religion and self-help Christianity of no use.

> I could not retreat, as did so many, into the church and its mysteries. My parents rejected all dogmas. We spurned the holidays marketed by the people who wanted to be white. We would not stand for their anthems. We would not kneel before their God. And so I had no sense that any just God was on my side. "The meek shall inherit the earth" meant nothing to me. The meek were battered in West Baltimore, stomped out at Walbrook Junction, bashed up on Park Heights, and raped in the showers of the city jail. My understanding of the universe was physical, and its moral arc bent toward chaos then concluded in a box.[1]

This literary irruption of the real follows Coates's remembrance from childhood of another young man threatening him with a gun. He writes soon after, "Fear ruled everything around me, and I knew, as all black people do, that this fear was connected to the Dream out there. . . . But how? Religion could not tell me."[2]

Look, our Beatitudes must encompass this reality. They must encompass all reality. The higher reality of Jesus and his gospel must speak into this prevailing mode of existence, or we shouldn't expect anybody anywhere to give two cents for our Christianity.

But this reality is exactly what the Beatitudes are acknowledging and encompassing. We may have them painted in calligraphy on some lacquered cutting board hung on Grandma's wall, but they belong in West Baltimore, Walbrook Junction, Park Heights, and the city jail, for that is the reality Jesus was stepping into.

The real Jesus grew up in a specific culture where his specific body was in varying states of danger. In his world, those representing the place of privilege could pull you over, detain you, take your property, effectively lynch you, make of you an example, and suffer no recourse when all was said and done.

Like so many marginalized peoples today searching for some shred of dignity in their ancestry, Jesus's people had a proud heritage that was a distant thing, an old story transmitted down a waxed line and echoing tinny in a hollow can.

Nobody quite knew what to do. There was no "Jewish culture," really, just like there is really no "black community." Who are you talking about?

There were some of Jesus's people who urged revolt. Most surrendered their aspirations in the face of ridicule or reason, but any who took it seriously ended up on a tree.

Some of Jesus's people—the Sadducees—acquiesced to the dominant culture, playing their assigned roles and compromising. Their own people considered them sellouts, clowns, "house Jews."

The marginalization of Jesus's people was mainstream. They lived lives of mostly quiet desperation in the land that once was theirs.

And when Jesus began his messianic ministry, he did not avoid any of this. He took the full weight upon his back and shoulders and buckled under it. He dove into it. He went around throwing it in everyone's face, drawing the circumference of the universe around it with himself at the dead center.

And in the end, they put him on a tree too.

Jesus wasn't blowing smoke. His major contribution to the world was not a set of aphorisms. He was born in a turdy barn, grew up in a dirty world, got baptized in a muddy river. He put his hands on the oozing wounds of lepers, he let whores brush his hair and soldiers pull it out. He went to dinner with dirtbags, both religious and irreligious. His closest friends were a collection of crude fishermen and cultural traitors. He felt the spittle of the Pharisees on his face and the metal hooks of the jailer's whip in the flesh of his back. He got sweaty and dirty and bloody—and he took all of the sin and mess of the world onto himself, onto the cross to which he was nailed naked.

In his work and in his words, Jesus is making promises to the beaten, the torn, the broken, the depressed, the desperate, the poor, the orphan, the abandoned, the cheated, the betrayed, the accused, the left-behind.

He is, believe it or not, promising to fix it all.

At the End of the Rope, Jesus

Obviously this stuff isn't fixed yet. We can see right now that it isn't fixed. Ta-Nehisi Coates sees it isn't fixed; he doesn't even seem to know if it *can* be fixed. Your neighbor across the street tries not to think about it, but when he's alone with his thoughts he suspects it can't be fixed either.

Our discipleship has to deal with this tension—the tension between the glorious reality we believe in and yearn for and the hard reality we currently live in every day—or else it's not the real Jesus we're following.

So here we are sitting in the dark.

Maybe you and I are sitting across from each other. Maybe I'm discipling you. Maybe you're discipling me. Or maybe we just found ourselves thrust together in this cave, helping each other untangle wounds from sins like monkeys picking nits from each other's fur. We need that monolith, man.

What if in our moment of utmost desperation—track with me here, if you can—at that moment where we've come to the end of our rope, we find Jesus?

I tend to believe that most of us do not truly treasure Jesus until we've run out of alternatives to him, until every last option has turned up dry. And think about this: What if Jesus actually brings us to the very moment of these no-more-rope situations in order that we might actually, finally trust him?

I mean, what if he called us dogs?

And Jesus went away from there and withdrew to the district of Tyre and Sidon. And behold, a Canaanite woman from that region came out and was crying, "Have mercy on me, O Lord, Son of David; my daughter is severely oppressed by a demon." But he did not answer her a word. And his disciples came and begged him, saying, "Send her away, for she is crying out after us." He answered, "I was sent only to the lost sheep of the house of Israel." But she came and knelt before him, saying, "Lord, help me." And he answered, "It is not right to take the children's bread and throw it to the dogs." She said, "Yes, Lord, yet even the dogs eat the crumbs that fall from their masters' table." Then Jesus answered her, "O woman, great is your faith! Be it done for you as you desire." And her daughter was healed instantly. (Matt. 15:21–28)

Jesus is extraordinarily merciful to those at the bottom of the barrel. This woman has come needy and vulnerable, and she is admitting her shame. She really has nothing to lose. It's desperation that makes her so bold, and Jesus knows it.

Their back and forth certainly looks cold. In calling her a dog, Jesus is basically affirming the ages-old relationship between Israelites and Canaanites begun way back in Genesis 9. But the woman's circumstances are deeper than that divide. Her sense of brokenness goes all the way down to Genesis 3.

And she owns her shame. She admits her poverty. She knows she deserves nothing. Yet she pleads for favor:

"Lord. Help. Me."

This is a prayer Jesus will answer. There are no strings attached, no caveats, no power plays, no manipulation, no guilt trips, no claiming of rights. Simply "Lord"—acknowledging that he is God and she is not—and "help me"—expressing her need by laying it at Christ's feet.

"Great is your faith," Jesus says.

Maybe you have struggled with great shame over some things in your life. Maybe you have sins that come back to haunt you, recurring sins in your life that you can't shake, or habits hard to break, or rumors from others about your history, or problems that persist to this day for sins you long ago repented of. That's some of the hardest stuff, isn't it? You've confessed, you've repented, you've moved on, but the shame persists. Maybe it's the consequences of your sins that are daily reminders of your past and regular temptations to doubt that you're forgiven. Or maybe you've got constant accusers throwing your sins back in your face.

You need to hear the gospel words of Zephaniah 3:19: "I will save the lame and gather the outcast, and I will change their shame into praise."

You need to hear the promise of Romans 10:11: "For the Scripture says, 'Everyone who believes in him will not be put to shame.'"

Why? Because Jesus Christ went to his death on the cross, "despising the shame," as Hebrews 12:2 says, enduring its agony in the full blazing weight of the wrath of God, that you might be forgiven and covered and secured and *free*.

Colossians 2:15 says, "He disarmed the rulers and authorities and put them to open shame, by triumphing over them in him."

He puts the shamers to shame!

What Jesus has done is good news for losers!

What Jesus has done is good news *only* for losers. If you're not a loser, in fact, you can't have Jesus.

If you are still dealing with shame, you need to know that when you have come in faith to the Lord for forgiveness, your sin has been paid for by the blood of Jesus on that cross, where he was hung naked, receiving your shame in front of everybody, including those who tortured and mocked him and made jokes about him. And when you come in faith to the Lord for forgiveness because of his cross, not only does he pay for your sin, forgive your sin, and throw your sin into the void to forget it forever but he now responds to you with delight. His eyes don't narrow at you, glowering. He's not sizing you up. No, his eyes sparkle at his children.

Ray Ortlund writes:

> Every one of us knows the shame of guilty self-awareness and the fear of exposure. But we don't want to live in the isolation of that darkness. We long for freeing relationships with others, especially God. But without the gospel, we hide,

conceal, falsify ourselves, in order to appear better than we are. Or, conversely, we may trot out our failings with assertive self-display, demanding acceptance—a more modern response.

The gospel says, "Your shame is real, even more real than you know. But this is what God has done. He put it all onto Christ at the cross, where your Substitute was utterly shamed and exposed and condemned for you. Now your shame no longer defines you. What defines you, what reveals your future forever, is this word: '. . . adorned. . . .' Not shamed. Adorned. Lovely. Attractive. And the moment is coming when he will look into your eyes with glad adoration, and you will look into his eyes with confident surrender. And nothing will ever, ever spoil it again."[3]

In Genesis 3, Adam and Eve realize they are naked and become ashamed, and they try to cover themselves. But God says their efforts at self-cover aren't good enough and he covers them himself with the flesh of sacrifice.

What a great God we serve! Rich in mercy and abundant in loving-kindness. Visiting grace from generation to generation according to his steadfast love. His gospel endures forever!

When we turn the Sermon on the Mount—or any of Jesus's teachings, really—into a handy compendium of pick-me-ups for spiritual go-getters, it proves we don't get it. It proves we don't get the gospel.

What is discipleship, then, but following Jesus not on some religious quest to become bigger, better, or faster but to become more trusting of his mercy toward our total inability to become those things?

When Jesus calls you a dog, in other words, you don't argue with him—you own your dog-ness.

It's those who would find this admission beneath them, who think themselves above Christ and his gospel, actually, who will end up losing in the end.

Those who get to the end of the rope, though? Those so overwhelmed they've run out of angles to play, formulas to recite, motivational posters to quote? Those who perennially "cannot even"? Those who sit in the dark wondering how, when, why, and where to start looking for the light? Those who are desperate for Jesus, no matter the cost (mainly because they've already lost it all)?

Winners, the lot of 'em.

3

Staring at the Glory until You See It

(When You Struggle to Believe Beholding Is Better Than Behaving)

> I see my light come shining from the west unto the east. Any day now, any day now I shall be released.
>
> Bob Dylan[1]

My gospel is smudged. It doesn't seem at first glance much to look at. If I had inadvertently dropped it on the sidewalk, you might step over it like you would a penny. Who stops for a penny?

Quick: Without looking, can you name the word imprinted on our one-cent piece to the left of Abraham Lincoln's profile? Do you know which way Lincoln is facing? On the "tails" side of the penny is an image of what? Don't say "a building." Which building? To the right of that building, there are initials. What are they? Whose are they?

Look, you know what a penny looks like. You probably see one every day, but I bet you couldn't answer all of the questions in the previous paragraph. Why? Because we don't really *look* at the things we think we already know. We don't study the familiar. The very fact we consider something *familiar* sort of stifles any impulse to study it.

I think this is the big problem disciples of Jesus have with the gospel. I think this is the big problem disciples of Jesus have *with Jesus*. We take him for granted.

In John 1:16, the apostle tells us that the fullness of Jesus provides "grace upon grace." I love that phrase. John tells us that Jesus is some kind of spiritual subterranean hot spring, bubbling up healing water through the icy ground. The reservoir of blessings in Jesus never runs dry. For all eternity, he is a fountain of life running free, overflowing, spilling over levies and dams, flooding our hearts—and eventually the entire earth (Hab. 2:14)—with the boundless radiance of his majesty.

And yet our ordinary image of Jesus is like that penny. We know what he looks like. Don't we? The portrait of Jesus in my mind is like that gospel in my pocket, dreary with fingerprints from use and yet somehow still inexhaustible and surprising. It somehow fits in the palm of my hand and at the same time circles the cosmos.

One of the subtle dangers of the way many Christians "do discipleship" is that they are always somehow looking at Jesus and yet never really seeing him.

This is why one of my favorite Bible words is *behold*. It's an important word. And it's—in my estimation—a significant improvement upon the more ordinary *look*. Some Bible translations do not include the word *behold* and instead use *look*. And while I'm not a textual scholar or any kind of biblical linguist and therefore have no idea what I'm talking about, I think this is wrong. (Being ignorant of something has never really stopped me from having an opinion about it, you see.)

> So I have looked upon you in the sanctuary,
>   beholding your power and glory. (Ps. 63:2)

> Then he brought me by way of the north gate to the front of the temple, and I looked, and behold, the glory of the LORD filled the temple of the LORD. And I fell on my face. (Ezek. 44:4)

> Behold, the Lamb of God, who takes away the sin of the world! (John 1:29)

> And we all, with unveiled face, beholding the glory of the Lord, are being transformed into the same image from one degree of glory to another. (2 Cor. 3:18)

Reread those verses without the *behold*s. Replace them with *look* or *see*. Do they sound the same? Do they have the same import? Look—I mean, *behold*—I know that *behold* and *look* and *see* are essentially synonyms. I'm not trying to make a point about Greek or Hebrew translation work; I'm simply saying that the word *behold* might be more helpful to the point of Christianity than an apparently perfectly fine alternative. John does in fact mean that his hearers should *see* the Lamb of God who takes away the sin of the world, but *behold* tells us what kind of seeing we ought to be doing.

In other words, he's not merely saying "look at him." He's telling us to look with consideration, with appreciation, with fixation and transfixion. To behold something is to "hold"

55

something in our vision, to let the weight of it rest on our mind and heart.

I love the story about the guy who was converted during a Charles Spurgeon sound check! He was apparently a workman in London's Agricultural Hall, where Spurgeon was preparing to preach later that evening. In those days they didn't have microphones or other electronic amplification systems, of course, so Spurgeon was testing the acoustics in the room. From the pulpit he bellowed John 1:29: "Behold, the Lamb of God, who takes away the sin of the world!" The workman heard it from the rafters and was struck to the heart, later seeking out more about this Lamb and his sin-taking ways, and coming to believe in Jesus.

From simply hearing the words of the gospel, this man beheld the glory of Christ in a profound way. He didn't just listen; he *heard*. He didn't just see the preacher; he in some real way beheld the Lamb.

And yet, while you can look without beholding—you can look at Jesus and not really see him—you can't behold without first looking.

We Are Starving for Glory

I believe I may be a distant relative of that woman visiting Jacob's well in John 4. Maybe I'm some descendant of a descendant of a descendant of one of her illegitimate sons. I don't know. I just *feel* that encounter as much as any other in the four Gospels. I can taste the gritty air on my tongue, feel the midday sun on my neck, sense the awkwardness of the invasion of that personal space. I think she just wanted to be left alone.

Can I get an amen?

I do like my personal space. Sometimes—okay, almost all the time—I just want to be left alone. (I'm writing these words at a coffee shop in Kansas City right now and I know about four people also currently in this coffee shop, and, not coincidentally, four is the same number of people I hope don't interrupt me while I'm writing.) When I was a pastor in Vermont, I used to take Wednesdays away from the church office and go work on my sermons in a local coffee shop that was in an old bank. They still had the vault, in which was placed one table. Can you imagine working in a vault? It was an introvert's dream.

There were some Wednesdays I'd get to the coffee shop early and would eagerly check to make sure the vault was clear, delighted to find it was. Then there were some Wednesdays I'd be running late and would approach the counter to place my order, then look to my right and see two feet sticking out from the vault doorway, and my heart would break. Somebody was in my vault! Other times I'd be the first to the vault and set up shop for the day, and later some total stranger—a clearly insane person—would enter the vault and sit at the table with me. Do you believe that? A total stranger! Trying to share the vault! (The audacity! The unmitigated gall!)

Really, nine times out of ten, I'd be totally cool with all of you people just leaving me alone. But here's lesson 4,036 that disciples of Jesus learn about their Master: when it comes to your personal space, he doesn't give a rip.

So I'm picturing this poor lady approaching the well. We have some evidence that she wants to be alone, not the least of which is that she's visiting the well at noon, which is pretty odd. Most people would go to draw water in the cool of the morning or the cool of the evening. You don't go get water in the hottest part of the day. At least, you don't do that unless you're assuming nobody else will be there.

But it's not simply introversion that has this lady at the well at high noon. It's more than likely the specter of her past—and of her present. As Jesus reveals prophetically to her, she has not a little bit to be ashamed of. And yet we know, just like Jesus did, that her shame is not entirely self-earned. She has likely been taken advantage of, used, and abused by all those men in her relational history. Even the current shack-up she's engaged in is not exactly comparable to the typically egalitarian cohabitation common today, as women in first-century Palestine did not fare too well on their own.

So I imagine that she has planned her visit in such a way as to be left alone, and here is this Jewish man just standing there as if waiting for her. And if the discomfort of sharing her personal space with this man isn't enough, he wants to have a conversation. Of course, Jesus speaks first. And he doesn't (apparently) say "Hi," or "How are you?" or "Fine day out, isn't it?" or "How you like them Mets?" but rather gives her an order. "Give me a drink," he says.

Don't believe the portraits of Jesus you got in your sweet little Sunday school class, where he's kind of shy and unassuming and would totally love to save you if, you know, it's not much of a bother to you. He's just kind of hanging out on your stoop with his hat in his hand hoping you'll notice him and will let him in. No, what is happening at Jacob's well in John 4 is the real Jesus—and he's showing up where he's not invited and giving commands.

What's crazy about the command, though, is that it isn't customary for a Jew to ask a Samaritan (woman!) for a drink. Like she might have cooties or something.

She mentions this. And Jesus sort of says, "Well, really, you should be asking *me* for water."

And now she's really confused and probably thinks he's a little *not right*. "How are you going to give me water when you don't even have a bucket?" she asks.

I'm paraphrasing, of course, but what ensues is a short conversation in which the Samaritan woman keeps trying to take Jesus's words in a different direction, staying on the surface—of religion, of politics, of culture—the way many religious people still do today, and Jesus keeps refocusing and drilling down. Eventually, like he does with the Canaanite he's called a dog, Jesus exposes this woman's greatest vulnerability. But not to shame her. No, not to shame her. The blunt, direct, command-giving, merciful Jesus brings her shame to the surface in order to cover it.

It's interesting how often the areas of our inner selves we strive the most to hide from Jesus are the ones he's most interested in. And it's amazing that these things about ourselves we hope he doesn't see are the very things he means to cover with his grace.

Adam and Eve hid from God and tried to cover themselves with fig leaves. It wasn't that God didn't want to cover their shame. It's just that he wanted to cover their shame with a sacrifice. Their covering was superficial. His covering was costly. He did not plan to leave them naked and afraid. But to cover them rightly, something had to bleed.

This poor lady—my great, great, great, great aunt—has just come for refreshment. And Jesus comes to offer her restoration. She's shifting around the fig leaves; Jesus is eyeing the sacrifice.

You and I come to Jesus looking for some kind of pick-me-up, and Jesus offers his flesh. We come looking for Jesus the life coach when what we really need is his glory. We need to *behold* him.

This is really the point of following Jesus—to become like him. And in order to become like him, as Paul says in 2 Corinthians 3:18, we must behold his glory.

But we keep stepping over his glory on the sidewalk. We won't even stoop to pick it up. It seems of little worth at first glance. Our faculties are not trained to stagger at this worth we are seriously and sadly misjudging.

It is often right in front of us, like Jesus face-to-face with the woman at the well. "If you knew the gift of God, and who it is that is saying to you, 'Give me a drink,' you would have asked him, and he would have given you living water" (John 4:10). We don't even know what we're thirsty for!

This woman was parched. She was starving. She was thirsty and hungry—for glory. She didn't know it when she walked up but she knew it when she left. (Thank God Jesus doesn't respect our personal space. Nobody would ever get saved if he did!)

We are parched. We are starving. We are thirsty and hungry for the glory of Jesus.

Every day when you encounter God—in your devotional time, in your time of worship, in your community groups or classes, or in any other moment in which you spend time with Jesus—you face the choice of simply looking at Jesus or actually trying to *see* him.

Get Right on Out

The problem is that many Christians have stifled their ability to behold the glory of Christ without realizing it. They have stunted their capacity to see some measure of his all-encompassing excellencies, not because they are generally disinterested in him but because all of their other interests have dulled their spiritual senses. All of the other things they look at dull their vision. They struggle to behold Christ's glory because they have a generally decreased capacity for bigness in the first place.

But we can work against this. We can do some simple things that help us behold better. What efforts can you make to help yourself behold the glory of Jesus?

Well, maybe you want to start by going outside.

Think of the steward in C. S. Lewis's illustration who has escaped the intramural political debate among his shipmates by "taking a breather" up on deck:

> For up there, he would taste the salt, he would see the vastness of the water, he would remember that the ship had a whither and a whence. He would remember things like fog, storms, and ice. What had seemed, in the hot, lighted rooms down below to be merely the scene for a political crisis, would appear once more as a tiny egg-shell moving rapidly through an immense darkness over an element in which man cannot live.[2]

Truly, I think one reason we aren't captivated by Christ's glory is because we have a diminished capacity to be captivated by anything big. We are preoccupied with small things. And, in fact, we somehow have an inverted sense of measurement in that big things seem to us small or familiar while small things become big to us, at least in terms of our time and attention and energy. It is the fun-house mirror–effect of daily living in a consumeristic culture where we are inundated with all kinds of media and now even carry that media around in our pockets along with our gospel and find ourselves pulling out that media more often because we sense there will be something newer, more vital, more exciting, more entertaining, more applicable to our situation somewhere among its endless clicks and pages, while that gospel seems so one-note and familiar. Our screens give us a constant stream of things to look at but very little to see.

Then we do eventually pull that gospel out and, well, it looks a little smudgy, doesn't it?

So here's what we need to do: turn some things off. Put some things down. Don't just do something, sit there.

I can't tell you how profoundly *settling in God* it is for me at the end of a day in the study, in meetings at the coffee shop, in the pixelated trenches of Word docs and social media feeds to go out on my back deck and sit and stare at the mountains.

I know, it's weird.

Once I took my daughter and her friend shopping at a local outdoor mall. I dropped them off and then went to the coffee shop in one of those big chain bookstores. I read a little bit from a book, and I confess I looked at my phone a little bit, but when I looked up, I felt self-conscious because everyone else was looking at their phones. I decided to just sit there and think. I did some people-watching. I drank my coffee. But I kept my head up and my mind active. I did that for about an hour.

When my daughter and her friend finally found me, my daughter walked up and said, "You look weird."

"Why?" I asked.

"Because you're just sitting there."

Apparently "just sitting there" looks weird. It was a strange sight to her to see someone sitting out in public who wasn't looking at a screen. Or looking at anything in particular. She thought, in fact, it seemed a little creepy that I was just sitting there. That's how upside down we are.

But until we learn to simply sit there, to be still, to be settled, to look at the great big world around us, to consider with wonder all these incredible humans made in God's image, to look at his endlessly fascinating creation in long, steady concentration, we will continue in spiritual myopia and spiritual boredom. When our vision is constantly occupied by small things, we are tempted to yawn more at the glory of God.

We have to look at big things in order to increase our capacity to see big things.

Here is John Piper on why staring at the sky helps guard against lust:

> Do you know why there are no windows on adult book stores?
> . . . Because they don't want people looking out at the sky.
> . . . The sky is the enemy of lust. I just ask you to think back
> on your struggles. The sky is a great power against lust. Pure,
> lovely, wholesome, powerful, large-hearted things cannot
> abide the soul of a sexual fantasy at the same time.
>
> I remember as I struggled with these things in my teenage
> years and in my college years . . . one way of fighting was
> simply to get out of the dark places—get out of the lonely
> rooms. . . . Get out of the places where it is just small—me
> and my mind and my imagination, what I can do with it and
> get to where I am just surrounded by color and beauty and

bigness and loveliness. And I know that when I used to sit in my front yard at 122 Bradley Boulevard with a notepad in my hand and a pen trying to write a poem, at that moment, my heart and my body were light years away from the sexual fantasizing that I was tempted by again and again in the late night, quiet, secluded in-house moments. There is something about bigness, something about beauty that helps battle against the puny, small, cruddy use of the mind to fantasize about sexual things.[3]

Do you want to see glory? "The heavens declare the glory of God" (Ps. 19:1).

Resting from the spaces, then, where you are an acting sovereign and instead getting out into the spaces where God's sovereignty is more palpable, believe it not, will help you see Christ as *bigger*.

See, what you're focused on will shape you, lead you. The spiritual dynamic the apostle Paul is employing in 2 Corinthians 3:18—how beholding Christ is in a way becoming a likeness of Christ—works for almost anything else we're intently looking at. What we behold, we in some way become.

G. K. Beale says, "What people revere, they resemble, either for ruin or restoration."[4]

Want a heart as big as the sky? Behold the sky.

Want a soul as bright as day? Behold the day.

Or, alternatively, if you want a shriveled heart panting for satisfaction, just keep staring at the ceaseless parade of the detritus of our shortsighted culture on your closest screen. Or simply maintain your vision of the ultimately inconsequential Jesus so fashionable in the world and in worldly churches.

What all this boils down to is this: we have, fundamentally, *a worship problem*, and so long as we are occupying our minds with little, worldly things and puny, worldly messages, we will shrink our capacity to behold the eternal glory of Jesus Christ, which is the antidote to all that ails us.

Beholding Is Better Than Behaving

I have shamelessly stolen the title of this chapter from my friend Ray Ortlund, who once exhorted his congregation to "stare at the glory of God until you see it."

Now, as I've already said, you can look without seeing but you can't see without looking. So we have to look. But the problem is that the way many of us are discipled trains us to look just a few degrees off the right point of glory. Like my early experiences in that Sunday school class so focused on making sure we all did our discipleship duty each week, checking all of our completed religious assignments off the list, it's not that what we're trying to do is bad. It's not a sin to want to obey God and, in fact, it's the very definition of sin not to!

But here's the problem: there's not enough glory in the commands themselves to help us obey them. There is a lot, but not enough. There's insufficient glory in the law of God to empower us to obey it.

This is another provocative idea Paul explores just before he lays out his life-altering claim that beholding the glory of Jesus is what actually changes us. By contrast, he's willing to say, focusing on the law cannot change us. The gospel is better than the law.

Now if the ministry of death, carved in letters on stone, came with such glory that the Israelites could not gaze at Moses' face because of its glory, which was being brought to an end, will not the ministry of the Spirit have even more glory? For if there was glory in the ministry of condemnation, the ministry of righteousness must far exceed it in glory. Indeed, in this case, what once had glory has come to have no glory at all, because of the glory that surpasses it. For if what was being brought to an end came with glory, much more will what is permanent have glory. (2 Cor. 3:7–11)

Paul is recalling the giving of the tablets of the law to Moses on Mount Sinai. As Moses would go up and commune with God, the glory of the Most High was so intense it would continue to radiate from his face when he came down. This radiant glory was so intense that Moses covered his face with a veil to shield the children of Israel from its intensity.

But as stark and intense and awe-inspiring as that glory was, Paul says, it is eclipsed by the ministry of the Spirit, the ministry of righteousness, the ministry of the gospel of Jesus.

The law is good and holy and necessary. The glory of the law is incredible. But the glory of the law is fading; it is passing away. The glory of Christ so exceeds the glory of the law, as Jonathan Edwards once said, it is like the sun rising in its strength and eclipsing the stars.[5] In verse 11 Paul describes the glory of Jesus revealed to us in the gospel as "permanent," implying that the glory of the law is somehow temporary. If you think about it, we won't need the law in the new heaven and the new earth, because there will be no more sin to restrain, no more curse to adjudicate, no more death to administer. But the glory of Christ? It will be the virtual sun of the new heaven and the new earth, enlightening all the restored creation with its cosmic beauty.

Yes, the gospel is better than the law. And yes, in fact, beholding is better than behaving.

This is why, as odd as it sounds, making your entire Christian life about trying to look like a good Christian is a great way to become a terrible Christian. Or at least a weak and defeated one.

This is so important to understand. It is crucially important. It is so important that I want to violate a cardinal rule of sophisticated composition and employ every means of emphasis that I can to restate it:

YOU CANNOT GET POWER TO OBEY THE LAW FROM THE LAW ITSELF!!! POWER TO CHANGE CAN ONLY COME FROM THE GLORY OF CHRIST!!!

Man, that looks terrible. Please forgive me for that assault on the eyes. But it's an idea worth looking foolish to emphasize because it is so counterintuitive to the flesh, so *contra* the wisdom of the world—and *contra* most religious ideology—that it's worth writing it like some junior high school girl's tweet about Justin Bieber. This idea ought to be tattooed on our inner eyelids. And if you just happened to pick this book up in a store and flipped through it, this would be the one idea I'd want to catch your eye.

We think we know what will do the job of making us holy: us doing the job of making us holy. And seeking holiness is integral to discipleship. But more central to our discipleship is the news that actually makes Christianity *Christianity*: we are holy not because of what *we've* done but because of what *Jesus* has done.

This is why the good news is so good! The essential message of Christianity isn't "do" but "*done.*" The good news is *news*, not instruction, and it announces to us not "get to work" but "it is finished."

And so it turns out that the direct route to God-honoring behavior is born not of good behavior but of good beholding.

You'll Be Struggling to See the Glory Your Whole Life

I remember walking into an adult bookstore for the first time. (This was before high speed-internet connections were common and you could get the crack delivered to your home in five seconds or less.) I wanted to be there and yet I didn't. I was trembling inside and a little bit outside. When you walk into one of those places, you are clearly crossing a line, and it's as if that line demarcates a wall of glass. The porn shop is under a dome, keeping all the germs inside, and when you cross that boundary it slices you in half. If you're someone who claims to follow Jesus, you walk into a porn shop as a totally bifurcated person—divided, deluded.

I was *driven* there by a compulsion—to see things I shouldn't, to get things I shouldn't, to know things I shouldn't. There are sections inside an adult bookstore, organized according to category. I hope you didn't know that. Some of these categories repulsed me. Can you imagine that? Walking around a porn store and avoiding the "gross" stuff? As if it wasn't *all* disgusting?

I knew I should not have been there but I wanted to be. Everything inside of me said it was wrong, and everything inside of me also said it would be okay. *Just push through, get what you want, and get out.* Before you become numb to this battle and stop fighting it you must ignore the clapper of conscience clanging against the walls of your soul and push through it.

Was I in that store by my orientation? Absolutely. Was I in that store by my choice? Yes. The answer to this multiple choice question is *yes.*

And when I put Genesis 3:1 ("Did God actually say . . . ?") together with Romans 7, I see why I believed it was ultimately better at the time to feel good doing what I wanted instead of suffering the internal agony of not being who I was. It felt so much better to give in than to fight. Which is why so many porn users don't fight it at all. The porn promises release. The abstinence promises pain. And then there's this voice saying, *The pain means you shouldn't be trying to change who you are.*

But there's nothing else in me God wants to change *except* who I am.

This change comes through the cross—Christ's cross becoming my cross. What is better? To be warring all our life in Romans 7, denying our urges and not feeling good inside, or doing what we feel is right simply because it feels good, or at least better? One voice answers the latter, and it strokes the ear. The other strikes terror sometimes—okay, *many* times—but it takes us from Romans 7 to Romans 8.

Don't believe the lie that always struggling to obey God is a worse lot in life than disobeying him with peace. God did not make us to "feel good inside" (or outside) all the time this side of heaven; he made us to share in the sufferings of Christ, that we might also share in his resurrection. And the reality, for many, is that the resurrection kind of life in these areas of death isn't always postponed until the life to come. But you won't know that until you're willing to go to the cross for as long as it takes to die.

I was preoccupied with and perversely interested in pale imitations of glory. I was committing clear sins in engaging in this behavior. And staying away from the porn shop would have been a good decision to make. But it was the allure inside of me—the desire for the glory that was being falsely promised—that just avoiding pornography wouldn't kill. I didn't simply have a behavior problem but a belief problem, a worship problem. And what eventually served to cure my taste for this shiny death was not "getting my act together" but finally, truly seeing the glory of my crucified Savior.

In the warp and woof of this struggle every day, we cannot rely on the law to empower its own implications. We need the more glorious vision.

So long as we are living in the bittersweet limbo of Romans 7 through 8—*simul justus et peccator*, as the Reformers so nerdily put it in the Latin (righteous and at the same time a sinner)—we will be struggling to see the glory. We will always be fighting this battle. When I say it is better to behold than to behave, I do not mean that we are to be lazy Christians, ambivalent about personal holiness or about actively following Jesus. I just mean that our ability to actively and persistently follow Jesus will be centrally driven by our comprehension of his glory.

Beholding Christ's glory is the number-one directive for following Jesus. And, in fact, it's sometimes the only effort we lousy disciples can muster up.

I think of that fateful Sunday a young Charles Spurgeon got waylaid by a snowstorm into a little Methodist chapel where a guest preacher filling in at the last minute was making a plainspoken appeal from Isaiah 45:22—"Look unto me, and be ye saved, all the ends of the earth" (KJV). He was not a great preacher; Spurgeon presumed him to be "a shoemaker, or tailor, or something of that sort," and actually refers to him as "feeble" and "stupid,"[6] but he recalled the man's invitation thusly:

> Now lookin' don't take a deal of pains. It ain't liftin' your foot or your finger; it is just, "Look." Well, a man needn't go to College to learn to look. You may be the biggest fool, and yet you can look. A man needn't be worth a thousand a year to be able to look. Anyone can look; even a child can look.[7]

That Sunday morning, with snow clouding the view outside, this simple message captivated young Charles who, for the first time, looked at the glory of Christ and *saw* it.

Sometimes people are so busy trying to do great things for God they forget to look at his glory and therefore never quite behold it. And sometimes looking is all the rest of us have the energy for. We are, whether spiritually or physically, out of "get up and go." But as this "stupid" preacher reminds us, any ol' fool can pick his head up and look.

So how do we pick up our head and look so as to *behold*?

4 The Rhythm of Listening

(When You Think God Is Giving You the Silent Treatment)

This is the thankfull glasse, /
That mends the lookers eyes:
this is the well /
That washes what it shows . . .
Thou art joyes handsell:
heav'n lies flat in thee.

George Herbert[1]

My gospel is an old hymn. My gospel is sheet music printed in antiquarian typeface on a yellowed page in a dusty book. It's the "old, old story" and the "old rugged cross." My gospel is four verses—and please don't skip the third verse to expedite the invitation! My gospel is an invitation to a bygone time that feels new again, even in our age of ever-dawning progress and modernity. My gospel gets "dug up" and "trotted out" and sung ironically and apologized for by leaders too clever for their own good. But then it lands in the ears of those led as sweetly familiar, warms their souls like celestial comfort food, and always gets sung louder than those Jesus-is-my-boyfriend ditties.

At first glance, the gospel of the kingdom is not much to look at. We tend to take it for granted. It sits in the splintery pew rack of our imagination like some hallowed curiosity. And, when bored with the latest distractions, we happen to take it up again and turn to our favorite number, it's like coming face-to-face with an old friend. It's like we never neglected it. We pick up where we left off.

I notice this phenomenon every time I hear audiences sing actual hymns during congregational worship time. It's even noticeable at student ministry events, although you wouldn't expect it to be so. It is young people, we assume, who most find the old hymns musty. "They only want the new stuff," says the common wisdom. But I've spoken at more than a few student ministry events, and while most Christian teenagers seem engaged enough during worship music of all kinds, I hear the difference when some leader, immersed in the fog and lasers of newness, "dusts off" an oldie. The kids *sing*.

I notice this in plenty of other venues as well—at church services, men's retreats, and Bible conferences. Why is this?

I don't think it's just because hymns are familiar. These audiences know the new stuff too. In fact, the new stuff dominates the worship scene for a reason. I think the persistent resonance of hymns does have something to do with the fact that hymns—for church folks, anyway—are historically familiar. These old songs take us back to simpler, more formative times in our life of discipleship, and few things beat nostalgia for warming the heart. But I don't think it's simply nostalgia that makes the hymns so affectionately *singable*.

I think many of the old hymns, the ones that have endured—and plenty of the newer hymns too, actually—tap into a deeper reality than a lot of the more explicitly emotive stuff. In a strange way, the old gospel hymns affect us *more* emotionally by not dealing primarily with how we feel. There are plenty of emotional exclamations in the old hymns, of course—"How marvelous, how wonderful," "Then sings my soul . . . how great Thou art," "Amazing grace, how sweet the sound," and so forth—but these songs don't make our emotion the primary point. They make emotion the response to something much sturdier—namely, the gospel.

Most of these old hymns follow the gospel story line. The first verse usually presents the problem of sin in some way. The second and third verses typically introduce Christ and his cross, the work of the Spirit, or some other proclamation of the redemptive narrative of the gospel. And the last verse typically puts the Christian in heaven, focusing on the blessed hope of Christ's return and our glorification.

The classic hymns, like the gospel they help us exult in, are much bigger than they appear.

This is why I say my gospel is like the old hymns: I very often treat the gospel like something I've moved on from, but every time I bring it back to mind, every time I put my stupid little eyes on its familiar truths, it transports me to a more beautiful, more powerful, more helpful place than any of these newfangled messages I flirt with every day ever could.

A lot of the new songs—not all of them, of course, but a lot of them—head straight to how I feel about Jesus but never take me into the depths of why I ought to feel that way. We're summoning the wind, calling down the fire, pleading for rainfall. (I begin to wonder if I'm worshiping God or reciting some kind of medieval weather report.) I'm telling God what I want, what I need (what I *loooong* for, *ooooohh*).

But what I really need is to rehearse what he's already done for me, what he's already done in Christ that has satisfied my desires, met my needs, and answered my longings. In the rush to emotional outburst, I miss affectionate remembering.

Here, I'll tell you what it's like: the difference between a lot of modern, emotional worship songs and the classic, gospel-rich hymns is the difference between the romantic ruminations scrawled in a preteen girl's diary and the decades-long marriage etched upon the hearts of a tired-but-God-dependent husband and wife. We take our old marriages for granted too; they become too familiar to us, old hat. It is hard to muster up the romance of the newlywed days, well-nigh impossible to dig up the "twitterpation" of wet-eyed, dimple-cheeked courtship. In a hard-earned marriage between two survivors of the early mutual surprise that they married a more *sinny* sinner than they anticipated runs something deeper than mere feelings and stronger than flimsy romantic greeting card proverbs. In long marriages between two Jesus-followers we find a bedrock of true affection.

It's not for nothing that God categorizes the relationship between his Son and Christians as one between a groom and his bride. And in worship music just as in marriage, keeping the relationship fresh means frequently revisiting some old, familiar truths.

Getting in Sync with the Rhythms of Relationship

In the parlance of modern discipleship, we call the list of behaviors Christians engage in to develop their relationship with God "spiritual disciplines." This is a perfectly fine category. There's nothing wrong with disciplines, and certainly not with disciplines that are spiritual. Just like there is nothing wrong per se with the word *discipleship*, there's nothing inherently wrong with the word *discipline*. (They share a root, in fact, in the Latin word for *learning*.)

The problem, however, is in the modern evangelical's approach to these concepts. Disciplines can (and often should) be rigorous, and the cost of discipleship is, of course, taking up our cross (Mark 8:34). But if we are not careful, this rigorous, dutiful approach to the spiritual disciplines can begin to feel more about, well, *duty* than—oh, say—*delight*.

Many husbands and wives work hard to show their spouses love, but don't our spouses tend to hope that loving them doesn't feel so much like work to us? And don't we wish that for ourselves?

I don't know about you, but it hurts my feelings to know that it takes my wife a lot of effort to love me. I like to think I am incredibly lovable! But I'm not. I am hard to love. And I get harder to love the more of the real me you see.

But there is no sin in Christ. He is not like us. He is not unlovable. If we find it difficult to love Christ, the problem is not with him; it is with us.

This is, of course, where the spiritual disciplines come in. But what if we approached these behaviors less as religious duties—they are that, obviously, but they are more than that—and more as relational delights? What if the work we put into our relationship with Christ more directly flowed from our already-secured position in him than from some idea that we've got to maintain our spiritual state?

What if—in other words—we saw Jesus as our friend more than our boss?

Jesus is certainly our master. He is certainly our commander. He is our sovereign Lord, and thus when he says "Jump," we ought to ask "How high?" But our divine king also says this to his disciples:

> No longer do I call you servants, for the servant does not know what his master is doing; but I have called you friends, for all that I have heard from my Father I have made known to you. (John 15:15)

Of course, the fact that Jesus doesn't call us his servants doesn't mean we don't have to do what he says! It only means that our relational context for doing what he says has changed. He is not distant from us, some kind of divine CEO dispatching orders from on high via emailed memo. He is certainly our king and worthy of our total allegiance and submission, but he is also our older brother and our friend. This relationship, born of the gospel, helps us see that his commands come from a place of love and are positioned for our good.

And it helps us see that our obedience is not the grounds of our relationship but the overflow of it!

Again, discipleship is not about *not* obeying God. I am only trying to suggest that our motivation for obeying God is often off biblical center, and thus our efforts to stay close to God begin to feel more like work than worship.

Again, it's not about not working. To be gospel-centered is not to be law-avoiding. As Dallas Willard says, "Grace is not opposed to *effort*, but is opposed to *earning*."[2] So it's not about "letting go and letting God" or some other similarly sincere but shallow spiritual hooey.

So, how about you? Does your relational upkeep with the Lord feel more like discipline and less like delight? Are your spiritual disciplines off-center? Are they off-gospel?

You know, there are some parts of the Bible that sound awesome until I realize I don't understand them. Once I realize I don't understand them, they don't stop being awesome, of course. But my awe is less of the "Wow!" variety and more of the slack-jawed, drooling "Ummm . . ." variety. Ephesians 5:18 is a prime example. Paul writes, "And do not get drunk with wine, for that is debauchery, but be filled with the Spirit."

The "don't get drunk" stuff I totally understand. Tell me not to do something, and I can usually handle it. It's the other part. "Be filled with the Spirit." It tells me to do something—which is great—but what exactly I'm supposed to do, I have no idea. How do I go about "being filled"? Doesn't the Spirit fill?

How do I *be* something the Spirit does?

It sounds as though Paul is telling me to get active about being passive. And in a way, he is.

I wrestle with this. It hurts my brain. I worry it appeals too much to my flesh, to the very persuasive part of me that does not have to be told to be passive.

But this is a different kind of passivity. It's not laziness. And it's not inactivity. It's a passivity that's more about receptivity. If you can figure out the difference, it's really about working without *striving*.

Clear as mud?

I think, if you'll consider the difference thoughtfully, you'll see that you're more familiar with this concept than you realized. In fact, I'm willing to bet that you are already quite acquainted with the concept of active passivity. Or passive activity. Or whatever you want to call it.

According to the 2000 US Census, 79 percent of Americans live in urban or suburban areas. Most people who will read this book live in what we often simply call "the city" or in a suburb of the city. Every day those of us who live in these areas, particularly in the suburbs and the "nicer" areas of the city, demonstrate with our routines and our attitudes that we are experts at actively being filled with the spirit of *something*. It is deceptively and dangerously easy for even suburban Christians, because of the environment of convenience and consumerism they swim in, to become lovers of convenience and embracers of consumerism.

Where we live, and *how we live there*, shapes us. It does so with our participation and permission even though most of us are not conscious of it. And that is the same sort of active passivity Paul appeals to in the confusing part of Ephesians 5:18.

To be blunt: I think the spirit at work in the suburbs tends to smother the Christian spirit. I know this personally because I have spent most of my life there. The message of the suburbs, in a nutshell, is self-empowerment. Self-enhancement. Self-fulfillment. Self is at the center, and all things serve the self. (Self-service!) The primary values of suburbia are convenience, abundance, and comfort. In suburbia you can have it all—and you can get it made to order in a super-sized cup with an insulated sleeve.

Whether we realize it or not, the values of suburban culture affect us. They shape us. They slyly dictate how we think, how we act, how we feel. And how we follow Jesus. (Or don't.) The cultural tide of suburbia is exceedingly hard to swim against. Rather reflexively, we feel we must have the nice house for our busy family, the nice car to get us to our rewarding job, and the nice neighborhood amenities to make all of life more livable. And for followers of Jesus it becomes exceedingly difficult to engage in worship of him that goes beyond a weekend church service and invades the space and time of the rest of our "real life."

Most of us certainly make time for God when we feel we have the time, doing our best to fit him in somehow between the paths from house to car, car to work, work to car, and car to home. The problem is that God owns all of life, and worshiping God means we must revolve around him, not he us. So God shouldn't be confined to his own compartment in our schedule. Jesus does not abide in his assigned time slot; we abide in him.

But how do we do that?

What we are talking about here is the process of *formation*: allowing ourselves to be formed a certain way. Most of us have already done great at being formed by the consumer culture we're immersed in. We have adapted quite well to the rhythms of suburbia and even stuck a Jesus fish on some of them. To cultivate Spiritual* formation, then, means to find ways to immerse ourselves in the work of the Spirit—to *re-sync ourselves to the rhythms of the kingdom of God.*

Unfortunately these rhythms are difficult to hear and feel inside the noise of our consumer culture, which is blaringly loud even in the peace of the suburbs. Everything, from the

---

* I usually capitalize the word *Spiritual* when it describes some work of the Holy Spirit to remind myself and others that true Spirituality is not the experience of some amorphous, religious "force" but an encounter with the living God who is real and personal.

pace of life to the periodicals in the café newsstands, adds to the public noise drowning out our personal discernment of God's Spirit. The rhythm of listening to God in his Word gets frustrated by the distracting syncopation of the culture, like when the white people try clapping along to a song at church.

As "be filled with the Spirit" indicates, and as Jesus's command to "abide" (John 15:4) implies, there is an intentionality and active participation on our part. But the difference between the Bible's teaching on obedience that pleases God and so much of the church's teaching on obedience that pleases God is exactly where the relief of the good news comes in.

Did you, like me, grow up in a church environment that stressed things like quiet times, service projects, and worship services—which are all good things—in such a way as to create holy homework for the Christian life? If so, you've probably already felt the difference between relational rhythms and religious burdens along your Christian journey.

What was often missing from my own spiritual formation attempts in the past was the central place of the good news of Jesus's work, which is complete and sufficient. Imagine if Paul had simply written, "Work out your own salvation with fear and trembling" (Phil. 2:12). To stop there provides good, solid instruction, but there's not much good news in it. It is sufficient for Christian busywork, and by itself it would be great at creating more of what it requires. But Paul *didn't* end the thought there. He doesn't just say, "Get to work." He continues in verse 13, "For it is God who works in you, [enabling you] both to will and to work for his good pleasure."

Finally! Good news!

Perhaps we should think of "being filled with the Spirit" like we do about sailing. Did you know that there are roughly sixty working parts on a sailboat? There's plenty of work to do when sailing. You can break a sweat. You have to stay attentive. But there are two things you can't control on a sailboat, and they make all the difference in the world. No amount of elbow grease will (1) control the tide or (2) bring the wind. You can hoist the sail, but only the wind can make a sailboat *go*.

There are plenty of approaches to Spiritual formation that amount to teaching us how to row our own boat. Some put us in a sailboat but have us blowing deep breaths into the sail. Consequently many of us get really tired on the way to nowhere.

But what about those of us who were tired before Jesus even got to us? What about those of us who find ourselves constantly short of breath?

What is the use of telling a guy in bare feet to pull himself up by his bootstraps?

I mean, if you had a motor already, you wouldn't need the wind, would you? Unless your motor was broken.

Well, hopefully you've realized by now that this book is not for spiritual speedboat captains.

When Jesus hit the scene two thousand years ago, he preached "the gospel of the kingdom," which one could achieve access to by denying oneself. In order to experience life in this kingdom, Jesus said, one must "take up his cross"—one must, in some way, *die*. The beauty of this command is that it is, in fact, "easier" for those who already feel in some way dead to feel very close to the kingdom. (And the ugly truth of this command is that it actually makes it more difficult for people who feel like they already have their act together to see any appeal in Christ or his kingdom.) Those who live in a near-constant state of desperation are typically the ones most receptive to Jesus.

And Jesus proclaimed that his kingdom is specifically for those who could own their desperation. (This is why he praised the woman willing to eat crumbs under the table like a dog.) In the Spiritual economy of the kingdom of God, the lowly are made high while the high and mighty are brought low, the poor in spirit become rich while the rich see the hollowness of their treasure, and the hard-on-their-luck hear good news while the happy-go-lucky seem barely interested.

The Holy Spirit is committed to this glorious gospel inversion. He is committed to making sure that those who follow Jesus are becoming holy. Or, rather, the Holy Spirit is committed to making sure that those who are holy are following Jesus!

This, too, is good news: the Spirit who authors our faith will perfect it. The Spirit who justifies us will sanctify us, and the Spirit who sanctifies us will glorify us.

The Spirit who empowers our conversion will empower our discipleship.

With this gospel in proper perspective, followship of Jesus does not cease to involve effort. But it does place effort in its proper proportion to the true credit in our spiritual account. We are not holy because we work. We work because we are holy. If we don't get this order right, we don't get Christianity right. And we will always struggle with the so-called spiritual disciplines—struggle against them, even.

But if we center on the gospel, the essential duties of maintaining a relationship with God begin to seem less like duty and more like delight. They seem less like rules and more like rhythms.

Through the beautiful lens of this liberating good news, we'll look at the two most vital spiritual rhythms in discipleship to Jesus, beginning with perhaps the most important: listening.

Feel the Rhythm by First Listening to It

All right, what I'm talking about here is basically "reading the Bible." If you want to get technical, I should call it "studying the Bible." I have also often referred to this necessary rhythm of discipleship as "feeling Scripture."

I know using the word *feel* to describe a spiritual discipline seems weird, but for a long time I've looked for a better word and come up empty-handed. Don't let the word *feel* throw you off, though. It's not a particular emotional reaction you're looking for here, or a certain set of godly goose bumps or something like that. If you experience those things, that's great, but what "feeling Scripture" in this context means is a deeper familiarity with the message of the Bible, a sense of its big story line and a comfort with the diversity of its storytellers.

When I sleep someplace away from home, I almost always leave a light on. It's not because I'm scared of the boogeyman but usually because I'm scared of injuring myself if I have to suddenly get up because one of my daughters is crying or the phone rings or something like that. In an unfamiliar place cloaked in utter darkness, just getting up to use the bathroom can become a gauntlet of toe-stubbing horrors. But when I'm at home, utter darkness is good. It helps me sleep. And when I have to get up, it's usually no problem finding my way around because I know where everything is even if I don't see it. I have an innate sense of my nightstand's locale, of the bathroom door, of the dresser, and so forth. I can maneuver around and through these things in the dark because I'm used to doing so in the light. I never had to practice not running into things. I just had a daily routine that involved time in my bedroom. (And I didn't rearrange the furniture.) This is pretty much what I mean by "feeling Scripture."

Feeling Scripture entails regular inhabitance in the Bible—Jesus likes the word *abide*—so that we have a practically instinctual sense of its threads and contours. Getting to that place does involve reading God's Word over an extended period of time, but over time the effort we put into this practice begins to feel less like something carried out in our own power. What seems so unnatural and awkward before begins to feel more natural and reflexive.

My nightstand is an object of utility. It is to be used, not understood. (I am now picturing my nightstand on a psychiatrist's couch, which is just weird.) I don't look to my nightstand for the meaning of life (except when my Bible is inside its drawer). The problem with many of the ways we go about studying the Bible is that we treat it like an object of utility, not something that is life-giving and active. We read the Bible asking ourselves how we might use it rather than how it might use us.

So how do we stop "doing" when it comes to Bible study and start "being"? The difference is in how we read the Bible—how we *listen* to it.

The way we tend to approach God's Word is by looking for a purely informational exchange—to learn something. And the Bible has the wisdom of God in it, enough knowledge for a hundred lifetimes! But the primary reason to read the

Bible is not to learn stuff but to *be* stuff. Transformation is the primary reason the written Word of God exists.

Feeling Scripture requires discipline and consistency, like most Bible study plans do, but the aim of feeling Scripture is to treasure God's Word in our hearts and delight ourselves in God's laws. We have at our fingertips the very revelation of God to us, and yet we treat Scripture like a blunt instrument, like a dry reference book, like a prop for our propaganda, anything but the wellspring of God's truth to be drunk deeply from.

If we're going to look at following Jesus as "abiding in Christ," we have to dwell in God's Word. This means meditating on Scripture, chewing on it, and savoring it. This does not come easily at first, but the more we do it, the more natural it will feel. After a while, we will experience having been shaped by the message to automatically live the message.

But this all begins with simply listening.

It is an amazing thing that the God of the universe would refer to sinners like us as his friends.

Well, how can we be friends with God if we never listen to him? He has the answers we need to everything we face. His Word makes us complete, equipped for every good work (2 Tim. 3:16–17).

Heaven Laid Flat

In Psalm 119:103, David writes, "How sweet are your words to my taste, sweeter than honey to my mouth!" This is the testimony of someone who has come to thrive on God's Word, who has come to taste it and found it tastes really, really good.

I know that many times Bible study can taste like a stale rice cake. This is not because the Bible is not delicious but because our palate isn't developed enough to discover how delicious it is. But once we acquire the taste, we can't get enough of it. It creates more demand for what it supplies.

The more we dwell in Scripture, developing a greater taste and feel for it, the less sweet and less comforting the things of the world will taste and feel.

The wonderful thing about the Bible is that even as we develop our ability to find our way around in it, it never gets old or stale. "For the Bible," Martin Luther says, "is a remarkable fountain: the more one draws and drinks of it, the more it stimulates thirst."[3] Now, the Bible doesn't change, but when we develop a feeling for its revelation, our familiarity with it will nevertheless continually strike us afresh. It is as if God is constantly rearranging the furniture inside of it, showing us new things about himself and deepening our appreciation for his glory, but the more we discover this, the more prepared we are for the constant newness. The Bible is a book that teaches us how to read it as we read it.

The great British poet George Herbert wrote this poem about the holy Scriptures:

> Oh Book! infinite sweetnesse! let my heart
>   Suck ev'ry letter, and a hony gain,
>   Precious for any grief in any part;
> To cleare the breast, to mollifie all pain.
>
> Thou art all health, health thriving, till it make
>   A full eternitie: thou art a masse
>   Of strange delights, where we may wish and take.
> Ladies, look here; this is the thankfull glasse,

That mends the lookers eyes: this is the well
That washes what it shows. Who can indeare
Thy praise too much? Thou art heav'ns Lidger
    here,
Working against the states of death and hell.
Thou art joyes handsell: heav'n lies flat in thee.[4]

Herbert is not just describing the Bible here. He is *feeling* it! What is the Bible to Herbert? It is an infinite sweetness! It is a sweet morsel to suck on and savor. It is a delicious medicine, a tantalizing antidote. It is a mirror that both reflects our true sickness and at the same time heals us. It is a fountain whose water reflects our dirtiness and at the same time cleanses us.

What is the Bible to Herbert? It is "heaven laid flat." In other words, when we open up the Bible, it is like opening up a window into the divine world of celestial delights. It is a Word straight from God!

Clearly, how Herbert reads and responds to the Bible reflects what he thinks the Bible is. And what he thinks the Bible is impacts how he reads and responds to the Bible.

My primary walking-around Bible is an ESV journaling Bible. The binding is coming apart. I have written in nearly every margin. Some pages are crinkled and stained. There is a bloody fingerprint in there somewhere. (It might be chocolate, actually.) If you were passing by my green '97 Chevy Suburban in a parking lot and happened to see this worn-out book lying on the passenger seat, where it often rests, you'd hardly give it a second look. Certainly you wouldn't feel the least bit tempted to break in to my vehicle and steal this book.

But imagine somebody took you aside one day as you were walking by, grabbed you by the arm, pointed in the direction of my vehicle, and said, "Do you see that beat-up Chevy Suburban over there? On the passenger seat rests THE SECRET OF THE UNIVERSE."

Well, you might consider that for at least a second, wouldn't you?

The secret of the universe! The thing, the message that every human being has been searching for since the creation of the world. The skeleton key that unlocks humanity itself. The answer to all human desire and longing and dissatisfaction and brokenness. The very voice of God! A word straight from outer space! And it is inside that book inside that vehicle.

Well, if you really believed that the secret of the universe was inside that sorry-looking book inside that sorry-looking vehicle, you might linger a little longer at the window, wouldn't you? If you really believed this message, you might even smash the glass to get to that book.

But this is what we have! We have, in the book we call the Bible, the secret of the universe. This holy book contains, actually, the very Word of the very God.

And even though we have incredible access to this window into heaven—almost nobody in our part of the world has to break any laws to get access to the Bible, not like they do in some other countries—we just sort of *yawn* at it.

There is a spiritual reason for this, of course. Our hearts are still harder than they ought to be. Our flesh is not yet totally conquered. Our spiritual palate is not yet fully accustomed to heaven's store. It has a lot to do with the fact that we will always struggle to see the glory.

And it has a lot to do with formation. It has a lot to do
with how we've heard the Bible taught or how we've been
taught to study it ourselves. The delight's been sucked out
and pure duty has filled the vacuum. (Though obviously it's
better to read the Bible dutifully than not to read it at all.
The delight has a way of marching back in, even uninvited.)

It might seem like we are taking the long way around, but
being able to "feel Scripture" involves zooming out from the
mechanics of Bible reading and Bible study and seeing the way
the relationship between the messages we hear and the posture we hear them in affects us.

Listening to the Voice of God

Several years ago, one of the largest churches in North America, Willow Creek Community Church in South Barrington,
Illinois, bravely admitted, after a lengthy and expensive
spiritual survey of their community, that the process they'd
committed nearly twenty years to for forming fully devoted
followers of Christ wasn't working the way they thought it
would.[5] An extensive amount of institutional troubleshooting
ensued. As Willow Creek probed the spiritual lives of their
survey participants, they compiled a list of the most formative disciplines in the lives of believers they had identified
as the most mature, the most "Christ-centered." Do you
know what they discovered was the number-one catalyst for
spiritual growth?

> The common models of activating spiritual growth such
> as "getting people involved" in church activities (attending
> worship, participating in small groups, serving the needy)
> or sharpening their beliefs (salvation by grace, the authority

of the Bible, person of Christ) were helpful but not the most effective vehicles for producing evidence of spiritual growth. The most powerful "catalyst" for moving people through stages of spiritual growth, the survey revealed, was reading and reflection on Scripture.[6]

What was the most powerful discipline for real progress in friendship with God? *Listening to him.*

"My sheep hear my voice," Jesus says, "and I know them, and they follow me" (John 10:27).

This is the whole point of reading and studying the Bible—to encounter the glory of Jesus—and if we aren't reading and studying to encounter the glory of Jesus, we are missing the whole point. In fact, I suspect the struggles so many of us have in sticking with Bible study are directly related to our failure to listen and look for the glory of Christ there.

It's a very strange thing, this Bible; it's very mysterious. To see what we need to see, we have to hear what we need to hear. Many times we're looking without listening, and it just doesn't work that way.

Think of how closely connected not hearing and not seeing are in passages such as Matthew 13:13–15, where Jesus is quoting Isaiah 6:9. Consider how important proper healing is for real belief.

How then will they call on him in whom they have not believed? And how are they to believe in him of whom they have never heard? And how are they to hear without someone preaching? (Rom. 10:14)

Think of that strange parable Jesus told about the rich man and Lazarus in Luke 16:19–31, especially the part where the rich man, suffering in the torment of hell, suggests to father Abraham that the sight of a miraculous resurrection would convince his family to repent of their sin.

> But Abraham said, "They have Moses and the Prophets; let them hear them." And he said, "No, father Abraham, but if someone goes to them from the dead, they will repent." He said to him, "If they do not hear Moses and the Prophets, neither will they be convinced if someone should rise from the dead." (vv. 29–31)

Like the rich man, we assume that seeing is believing. But it turns out that hearing is believing. It turns out, actually, that to see we have to first hear. But to really hear we have to really listen.

This frustrates us. We want that visual. We want that miracle. We want to *see* things happening.

I know lots of people who complain about God's silence. As a pastor, I heard it more times in the counseling room than I'm able to count. "Pastor, I just feel like God is holding out on me. I'm talking to him, but he's not talking to me. God is giving me the silent treatment."

But so long as we have the Bible, this is simply not true. In fact, because we have the Bible, it is an incredibly selfish and sinful thing to say.

God's Spirit has breathed out his very Word, which was enough for the Son of God in the flesh to live on. It is enough to provide us everything we need for eternal life. And we complain for more!

Look, I do believe the Spirit speaks to Christians in other ways. I am not a cessationist. But the primary, most common, and authoritative way God speaks to us is in the Bible. And so we never lack for his voice, his guidance, his instructions, even his very will for our life (1 Thess. 5:16–18). How arrogant we are to hold this Bible we could never fully master in a million years, the book that contains the Word of God that stands forever, and think, *Yeah, but what else you got?*

Let's get the wax out of our ears. Let's tune our hearts to Scripture and look for Jesus there. If we do that, I suspect we will find "Bible study" much less routine, much less boring. Jesus cannot be boring.

And if we will do that, we will find that to read the Bible, to listen to the voice of God, is to huddle around a warm fire and a delicious feast and a flowing fountain of living water all at the same time. This book opened is certainly heaven laid flat. And the soul that is set on Jesus cannot encounter the language of heaven and not be changed.

Yes, the key to real power and growth is to somehow behold the glory of Jesus in a real encounter with him and his gospel. So it stands to reason that if we want our Bible study to change us—if we really want to feel Scripture in the way that ultimately matters most—we have to be looking for Jesus in the Bible's pages.

Luke 24 is one of my favorite chapters in all the Bible. It begins with the greatest moment in history, the watershed moment of great reversal: the resurrection of Jesus. This is the moment when all heaven breaks loose.

But in the immediate wake of that event, the fullness of its impact has not settled on all who knew Jesus. Some have not seen him yet. Two of his followers are walking to a village called Emmaus when Jesus shows up. They don't recognize him at first, and even though they have heard news of the resurrection, they still seem sad because they aren't sure if it's true.

Not only does Jesus confirm the news to them but he takes the long walk as an opportunity to preach the best expository sermon in all of history. Luke 24:27 tells us, "And beginning with Moses and all the Prophets, he interpreted to them in all the Scriptures the things concerning himself."

Jesus preached a message about himself, using the entire Bible.

What can we learn from this? That all of Scripture either points to Jesus's life and teaching or emerges from it. All of it.

To know God we must know Jesus. And to feel Scripture well we must see Jesus between its lines and at the beginning and end of its many trajectories. He is there, all over the place, and Christians committed to following him closely will seek the glorious enlightenment of the disciples on the road to Emmaus.

When you're in the Old Testament, wherever you are, ask yourself questions like, "What does this say about Jesus? How does this point to Jesus? Did Jesus ever quote or refer to this? What is the importance of this in the light of Jesus?" In the New Testament, finding Jesus in the Gospels is easy, of course, but making the Jesus connection in the Epistles is vitally important.

Scholar N. T. Wright says that we ought to read the New Testament as if Jesus in the Gospels is giving us sheet music for a masterwork symphony and as if Paul and the other New Testament authors are teaching the church how to perform it.

If you plan on keeping Christ at the center of your life, you must plan on keeping Christ at the center of your Christian practice, including your Scripture reading. Colossians 1:17

tells us, "And he is before all things, and in him all things hold together."

The point of the Christian life is not self-improvement or more Bible knowledge but *Christlikeness.*

What we are dealing with here, in the practice of the rhythms of the kingdom, is a worship of Jesus that declares he is the King of Kings and Lord of Lords. That truth should at the very least be reflected in the way we read the Bible. If he is before all things and holds all things together, he's probably in a lot of the Scripture passages we read regularly but don't take the time to see him in.

The message we receive from consumer culture is that we are the point—that we are the center of the universe and all things revolve around us. And when we buy into that it becomes very easy to think of our days as belonging to us, our finances as belonging to us, and even our spiritual lives as belonging to us. It's possible, in fact, to be "doing discipleship" in some very Christ-*uncentered* ways.

Therefore, how you come to the Word will help shape your capacity to see Christ's glory there. We see the glory of Christ most compellingly, most powerfully, most authoritatively, and most unerringly in his Word, but we have to look for Christ and his gospel there.

If you are simply reading the Word to check something off your religious duty list, to get some brownie points with the big man upstairs, to study for your next Bible exam, or to advertise your discipleship on Instagram, you will not get out of it all that you should.

The glory of Christ is actually blaring from the pages of the Bible. God is not only *not* giving you the silent treatment, he is practically *yelling.* The problem is not with his voice but with our ears. The more and harder we listen, however, the more of heaven's glorious music we will hear, and thus the more of heaven's glory we will see. And then our soul finds the rhythm of heaven.

Sure, you could describe this process like any way of making a practice into a habit—just "stick with it" long enough that it becomes natural and routine. And, okay, that will work. But it doesn't sound as exhilarating and intoxicating as your soul finding the rhythm of heaven, does it? And when the rhythm gets you, you bob that head. You don't even tell yourself to do it. It just happens. How could it not? The music is too good. You start to sing too. Even though you've heard the song a thousand times before and first from your crusty ol' grandma.

It starts with the rhythm of listening. But it results in praise.

5

The Rhythm of Spilling Your Guts

(When You Realize You're the One Giving the Silent Treatment)

What a man is on his knees before God,
that he is, and nothing more.

Robert Murray M'Cheyne

My gospel broadcasts on a different frequency. It communicates something subsonic, carried on wavelengths from hyperspace, too cosmic and too complex to be heard by a world stupid from noise. This is why, when I was a kid, I kept that tract in my pocket but burned up a lot of vocabulary on comic books, football stats, and Schwarzenegger movies.

Once, on a visit to Nashville, I found myself newly arrived at the airport, en route to baggage claim and on one of those conveyor belt walkway things—which always reminds me of *The Jetsons*—stuck behind a guy who was just along for the ride. I wanted to walk. He wanted to hog the walkway, oblivious to the world around him, and noodle on his BlackBerry. I was aggravated. I couldn't pass him, and he couldn't see me behind him because his nose was in a gadget. But even though I was getting irritated, I was still too much of an introvert to actually say, "Excuse me," or anything like that. I preferred to stew.

I grumbled in my mind. *Who does this guy think he is? What a jerk! He's taking up the whole walkway. Does he think he owns it? How selfish can he be? He's so oblivious. I'm trying to get somewhere! The middle of the walkway is no place to just hang out. What a self-absorbed moron!*

Then it hit me. And by "it" I really mean *he*, the Holy Spirit, in a lightning-quick heart smackdown of conviction. *Hey,* you're *being a self-absorbed moron*, the Spirit said. The truth is, I wasn't on a deadline. I was going to baggage claim, not trying to catch a flight. I wasn't trying to beat a clock. I wasn't transporting an organ for transplant. I was just doing what I always do: hurrying. For no good reason. And the whole time I was annoyed with the guy in front of me for acting like the world revolved around him, I was acting like the world revolved around me, as if this guy should just know that I want to get somewhere quickly and adjust his pace accordingly.

It's bizarre what hurry can do to us. I can blame this on my personality because I'm a pretty nervous, neurotic guy, but my personality does not bear all the blame. The pace of life in industrialized America whispers insistently every day, *Hurry up!*

Because of my naturally busy heart and the abnormally hectic pace of daily life, I find it increasingly difficult to be still. Advertisements tell me to "Act now!" as Facebook and Twitter keep me up to the minute on what everyone else is doing or thinking, and fast-food restaurants encourage me to procure and eat food quickly. My email inbox and calendar always remind me of my obligations and assignments. Television news bombards me with boxes and banners and tickers, a continuous feed of several ever-morphing headlines at once. They just want me to be informed. I am drowning in noise and it all makes me anxious. Chances are it has the same effect on you.

One little verse in the Bible cuts through the clutter, the noise, the stress, the dutiful obligations, the mismanaged priorities, the rushing, and the busyness and offers me an antidote to what ails me: "But he would withdraw to desolate places and pray" (Luke 5:16).

I like the word choice of the NIV, which renders the phrase "lonely places."

As I type these words right now my legs are bouncing. Why? Because I find it incredibly difficult to be still. I am sick. I'm a jumpy person. No place I have lived helps with this. When I was in the bucolic havens of rural Vermont, I was constantly stressed out because of the responsibilities of pastoral ministry. Now that I have a "cushy desk job" in the suburbs of Missouri, I am still a nervous little twit.

Don't laugh. You probably are too.

Inside our homes we are buzzing from television, tablets, laptops, mobile phones, and combinations of all of the above and more. Stress levels from homework and housework are at an all-time high. Even the drive to work, in cushioned, climate-controlled, and radio-equipped vehicles, is for many a great cause of stress. They don't call it the "rat race" and "the daily grind" for nothing.

Once upon a time in our not-so-distant past, experts predicted that with the rapidly increasing advances in technology, Americans would have a shorter workweek and so much time on their hands for recreation that they wouldn't know how to fill it. Well, we figured it out. We filled it up with more work and more busyness. The microwave doesn't create free time. It frees up time for us to fill with other things, and that's just what we've done. We may think watching television or surfing the web or playing video games is all leisure time, and oftentimes it is, but the constant connection to artificial noise—visual, aural, or both—gradually quenches our spirit. And the constant filling of idle hands with idol pleasures will result in our looking like the gelatinous masses passing for humans at the end of *Wall-E*, if not physically then at least spiritually.

Pastor and author John Ortberg writes, "We suffer from what has come to be known as 'hurry sickness.' One of the great illusions of our day is that hurrying will buy us more time."[1] Ortberg goes on to define clutter, superficiality, multitasking, and speeding up daily activities as causes of hurry sickness. One of the symptoms of hurry sickness, he warns, is the diminished ability to love those to whom we have made the deepest promises. Hurry sickness makes us too tired and too distracted to love well.

We immediately think of our family and friends, worried about what our hurry sickness may cost us in our relationships with them. But do we slow down enough to also think about what it may be costing us in our relationship with God?

Are you too busy "living" to enjoy abiding in Christ?

Too Busy, Can't Talk

God is calling us to rest in him regularly. But we cannot hear his still, small voice (or even his booming, declarative voice) because the volume on our routines is turned to 11. We are too busy listening to the gods of the world. Nor do we think to speak to him in much more than sound-bite prayers. We *can't* think to do so, because we don't make the time to think of much more than sound bites to say.

Hurry sickness means we are so awash in the noise of busyness that we compensate for it by accepting silence with God and loved ones.

The way I have tried to make up for neglect of prayer is to incorporate prayer into my life.

Sounds great, right?

And it can be. Surely if we are to pray without ceasing that means we should be praying while eating, reading, driving, paying the bills, watching movies, listening to music, reading blogs, exercising, and working at our jobs. We should bathe those activities in prayer, in part to keep ourselves tuned Godward throughout our routines and in part to better "take every thought captive" (2 Cor. 10:5) that can enter our minds during times of preoccupation or distraction.

But something significant happened to me when I attempted this sort of prayer practice apart from the practice of solitary, focused prayer. My prayers became somewhat mindless. My attention was divided. I did my best to keep my internal monologue directed toward God, but too often the result felt like taking God along for the ride on *my* plan for the day. He was not getting the overflow of watchful prayer in the crevices of my routine; all he was getting from me was what I could fit into the crevices of my routine. The outcome was hurried prayer. Prayer just became another thing to fit in. I wasn't feasting on God's presence but just giving him crumbs. I was multitasking prayer.

A 2009 Stanford University study published in the journal of *Proceedings of the National Academy of Sciences* revealed that concurrent uses of technology overload our mental capacity.[2] The results suggested that multitasking actually inhibits the very process we think it helps: efficiency. It turns out that doing several things and consuming several things all at once not only stresses the brain but also prevents us from doing tasks and understanding information with accuracy.

The spiritually ambitious among us may think adding prayer to our repertoire of multiple tasks helps us better engage spiritually, but when the only time we pray is while doing other things, we program ourselves toward spiritual distortion and relational imbalance with God.

In Colossians 4:2, Paul commands, "Continue steadfastly in prayer, being watchful in it with thanksgiving."

There are two aspects to this verse that are crucial to a proper rhythm of prayer: (1) continuing steadfastly in it and (2) being watchful in it.

Continuing steadfastly in prayer speaks to commitment, to routine practice, to endurance, and even to duty. *Being watchful in prayer* speaks to focus, clarity, and awareness.

You can be neither devoted to prayer nor alert in it if you do not commit to a time where you are doing nothing but praying. This practice is called intentional prayer.

Now, prayer is never really accidental; neither should it be incidental. Followers of Jesus need to commit to times of intentional solitude, with all artificial noises blocked out and adequate time to focus on talking to God scheduled in. As busy as we think we are, none of us has as large a burden placed on us as Jesus did. And even though Jesus was perfectly sinless, he still needed to disconnect, detach, and devote solitary time to the Father.

Here is that verse again, cutting through the clutter of haphazard multitasking prayer: "But he would withdraw to desolate places and pray" (Luke 5:16). None of us is better than Jesus. So if Jesus's intentional prayer involved withdrawal to deserted places, and he did so often, how awesome do we think we are that we don't have to follow suit?

Nobody can say with any integrity that they do not have time to do this. Nobody can say that they truly can't afford to do this. In all honesty, you cannot afford *not* to do it. Jesus apparently engaged in intentional prayer "very early in the morning, while it was still dark" (Mark 1:35). But maybe for you the best time is during a lunch break or in the evening. Let's not be legalistic about times or time frames but let's be devoted to prayer, to staying alert in it with thanksgiving.

Jesus himself commands this in Matthew 6:6: "But when you pray, go into your room and shut the door and pray to your Father who is in secret. And your Father who sees in secret will reward you."

Prayer as Spilling Your Guts

We see lots of descriptions and depictions of prayer in the Bible, prayers made publicly and privately, prayers of thanksgiving and of petition, prayers of hope and of despair, prayers of confession and of exultation, prayers of celebration and of mourning, but the words and actions of Jesus reveal that intentional, attentive, and solitary prayer is vital for a life of submission to the Father's will.

I think one of the primary reasons Christians do not make quality time for prayer is that they have been trained to think of prayer in legalistic terms of duty. I remember those two weekly Sunday school accountability questions that sent me on a direct-flight guilt trip every time: "Did you evangelize someone this week?" and "Did you have your quiet time every day?"

Evangelism and devotional times are not only important but also vital for the Christian life. But having these things framed (by well-meaning leaders) in the context of duty did not serve to make me crave time alone with God or evangelistic conversations with my friends. Instead I did them half-heartedly and fearfully, not out of love for God and neighbor but out of fear of having to turn in a bad report on Sunday.

Over time, the religious expectation of quiet times doesn't compel us to seek them out but rather tempts us to bristle under their burden. Even fifteen minutes, a blip on the radar of our day, seems too long and unwieldy for prayer, because we approach it as pure duty, not pure desire.

Nevertheless, it is true that to pray is our duty as Christians. There's just no getting around it. In Ephesians 6:18, Paul tells the church, "[Pray] at all times in the Spirit, with all prayer and supplication. To that end keep alert with all perseverance, making supplication for all the saints." And in 1 Thessalonians 5:17 he is even more to the point: "pray without ceasing."

There is no wiggle room in these commands to shirk our responsibility to pray. It is a command of God in Scripture. Clearly, though, regimented expectations have not worked to compel many of us to pray. What may work, however, is a rethinking of what prayer is and what it's for. If prayer is just another item on the checklist, it is easily abandoned because nobody grades us on it, nobody gives us a performance review about it, and it does not provide the immediate satisfaction of entertainment or other leisure.

In essence, we chuck prayer because the results of prayerlessness are not immediately felt or seen.

However, if prayer is not just another thing for the checklist but rather the thing that makes the checklist doable, and if we looked not for "results" in prayer but relationship, we might find it more appealing.

To put it bluntly: if there is a God of the universe (and there is), and this God of the universe loved you and wanted to be in relationship with you (and he does), wouldn't it be stupid *not* to talk to him? To put it more nicely, if the God of the universe is in control of our days and loves us enough to provide comfort and power for those who seek him, wouldn't prayer be the most important part of our day?

One of the reasons Psalm 46:10 says to stop fighting and know that the Lord is God is because when we are occupied with our daily struggles, we practically forget. Our life places our self at the center of the universe. As we juggle our obligations, complete our tasks, run through our schedules, and consume, consume, consume, we begin to think that *we* are God. And when that happens, prayer to the real God who covers us and cares for us seems superfluous. What's the point of telling God about the things you've already got covered, right?

Of course none of us explicitly says or believes this. But we believe it and say it with our actions and attitudes toward prayer. The duty of prayer becomes heavy and burdensome because we see God as an absentee landlord or a pleasant grandfather or a last resort.

But if we were to capture a sense of his greatness and wonder, of his all-encompassing might and love, of his fatherly goodness and his jealous zeal, of his eternity-spanning efforts to redeem us from sin and death through the gift of himself in the sacrifice and resurrection of his Son, wouldn't that make a difference in how we approach prayer? Or, rather, *shouldn't* it?

Where we once saw prayer as a religious act designed to merit God's favor (or the approval of other Christians), we now see prayer as an act of worship, done not to push God's buttons like he is some cosmic vending machine but out of response to his initiative in our relationship. This is why the rhythm of feeling Scripture comes first in this book. The expectation is that as you begin to wade into God's revelation of himself to you through his Word you will begin to experience the compulsion to reveal yourself to him in prayer—our second rhythm.

Worship is always our response to God's initiative. We do not of our own initiative seek him; he seeks us (Rom. 10:20). He speaks to us and declares salvation over us in the atoning and reconciling work of Jesus, and worship is our response to the instigation of salvation.

Lazarus was not wandering around his tomb like a zombie until Jesus said, "Over here, dude!" No, Lazarus was dead. Jesus commanded him to resurrect and come forth. In the same way, Jesus calls us forth into life, and prayer is how we find our way in the newness of that life. I'm sure Lazarus, newly risen, had to wipe the haze from his eyes and find his way out of the darkness of the tomb. Maybe he stubbed his toes a few times on the way out. It's okay if you feel like you're in the dark, if prayer feels like stumbling around and walking into walls. You're alive thanks to the resurrection of Jesus. And when someone saves your life, don't you feel it's your duty to thank them over and over again, in a way that is entirely different from the duty you feel to go to work or school every day, the duty you feel to pay your bills or go to the doctor for a checkup?

When we think of worshipful prayer as a duty, we can easily lose our taste for it. But when we think of duty as a worshipful prayer, the tables get turned on the entire concept of obligation. Prayer in its essence is simply that: daily explicit worship of the one who loves you more than anyone else does and saved your life as no one else could. Most of us have seen the difference it makes in a church service when the congregation appears as though they are there out of duty versus out of worship. The difference is typically the level of awareness of how amazing grace is and how good God has been. In the same way, intentional prayer is the daily, private worship service of those who are awake to the amazing greatness of the gospel.

And just as in the biblical depictions of worship—think David as desperate for the Lord as an animal dying of thirst or Isaiah becoming "undone" in the light of the blazing radiance of God's glory in the temple—our times of worship can strip us spiritually bare, expose our vulnerability, shrink us down to our proper proportion before God. And because we can't hide anything from the God who sees everything, we can be totally honest.

Before the holy God of the universe we can finally and totally be our real selves.

Look, prayer is spilling your guts. It doesn't have to be pretty. It doesn't have to be tidy. It doesn't have to be particularly eloquent or even particularly intelligent. But the Bible is how God speaks to us and prayer is how we speak to God. These two rhythms form the dynamic of our friendship with the God of the universe. You can't be good friends with someone you don't listen to, and you can't be good friends with someone you don't talk to. So we go about our personal devotions by studying the Bible to hear what God would say to us and then praying to God that he would forgive us for our hard-heartedness against his Word and empower us to understand it better and make it resonate more deeply in our hearts. Spilling our guts in prayer is how we process God's words to us. Prayer is how we interact with our friend Jesus.

And this friend never checks his watch when you're talking to him! You might. But he won't. He's not checking your prayer off his religious "listen to people" chore chart. He's not tapping his foot, looking over your shoulder for someone more interesting, or staring at his phone while you're vomiting up your latest experience in *the exact same struggle you've had for the last ten years.*

He is, in fact, more eager to listen than you are to speak. We go on and on about God giving us the silent treatment. "I just feel like God is so distant lately." In reality, it's always the opposite. We are constantly moving away, and he's constantly following. He is a much better chaser of us than we are of him. And he's a much better listener. He picks up everything. You don't have to repeat yourself, but it's totally okay if you do.

He's listening. Open up.

Pray Like This

Pray then like this:

> "Our Father in heaven,
> hallowed be your name.
> Your kingdom come,
> your will be done,
>   on earth as it is in heaven.
> Give us this day our daily bread,
> and forgive us our debts,
>   as we also have forgiven our debtors.
> And lead us not into temptation,
>   but deliver us from evil." (Matt. 6:9–13)

Of course, this prayer does not preclude any of the other examples of prayer or commands to pray found elsewhere in Scripture, but this particular snapshot communicates to us nonnegotiable content for kingdom prayer. If we prayed according to the kingdom of our self, for instance, we'd be concerned about our reputation and recognition, not God's. Our daily life communicates where our hope and trust is placed; we are actually "praying" with our words and deeds every day. Many of our prayers may look like this:

> My self on earth,
> Awesome is my name.
> My success come and my will be done.
> Give me lots of things I want (but think I need).
> Don't even think about debt (unless it's someone
>   else's).
> Don't worry about giving in to temptation, because
>   you deserve it.
> Deliver me from guilt anyway.

For this life is mine, and the world revolves around
me. Amen.

Okay, so that's pretty silly. But don't we live like that, or
at least fight the temptation to live like that, all the time?

Instead, Jesus models for us prayer that acknowledges our
dependence and weakness but largely takes our self out of the
equation. It is a prayer of emptied ambition and full hope,
which makes sense knowing that it is a kingdom prayer and
that the way into the kingdom is denying self and embracing crucifixion. What the Lord's Prayer is, then, is taking
the oars out of the water and raising the sail in anticipation
of the sure wind of the gospel of the kingdom. Even in its
opening line it has us cast our gaze above the dizzying fog
of the world and toward the kingdom of heaven.

The Lord's Prayer enlarges our vision beyond the overwhelming but really minuscule offerings of our noisy, idola-
trous world and shrinks our self-sufficiency to the point of
basic need. Kingdom prayer is prayer that is preoccupied
with God's glory.

That is how you find the rhythm of the kingdom in a consumer culture: by seeking the humility that comes from re-
jection of independence and admission of dependence and
embracing the confidence that comes from God's acceptance
of you through Christ.

In the words of Robert Murray M'Cheyne, "What a man
is alone on his knees before God, that he is, and no more."

Since prayer is acknowledged helplessness—spilling our
guts—the more we pray, the more we are abiding in the
strength of God alone. The more we pray, the more we are
surrendering thoughts of our own glory and the more we are
unbusying ourselves with the enterprise of our own glory.

Every day we are building our own Babel Towers, and in prayer we lay down our bricks and trowels and let God knock those towers down.

In prayer, we take on the right spiritual proportion—needy, helpless, dependent, faithful—that the glory of Christ might more fully fill us.

Holiness comes only from God. It is imputed in the righteousness of Christ to us and it is increased in the Spirit's sanctifying work. So we humble ourselves knowing this, and we pray prayers of thankfulness, requests for mercy, and pleas for more Christlikeness.

In enjoying the glory of the heavens, and especially in the meditation on the Word and supplication on our knees, we are seeking out Jesus. This is what it means to pray "In Jesus's name, amen."

I bet you've ended your prayers with that phrase many times. If you haven't, you have at least heard it prayed. What does it mean? Is it just a spiritual way to "sign off" from prayer, a way of saying "Sincerely" or "Yours truly"? What does it mean to pray in Jesus's name?

I have experienced no greater motivation in intentional prayer than encountering the incredible fact that Jesus Christ himself—God Almighty himself—is bearing my prayers to the throne room of Father God Almighty.

First Timothy 2:5 tells us, "For there is one God, and there is one mediator between God and men, the man Christ Jesus." This means that Jesus bridges the gap our sin creates between God and humanity, and because sin encompasses more than just our behavior but also our natural separation from God, and because Jesus's atoning work satisfies more than just the penalty of sin but also reconciles us to God, it means that his intervention covers both our weak prayers and our unprayed prayers.

I am not making this up.

Even better, not only does Christ's sufficiency cover the insufficiency of our prayer life, he himself is praying for us. Take a look at Hebrews 7:25: "Consequently, he is able to save to the uttermost those who draw near to God through him, since he always lives to make intercession for them."

Jesus's sacrifice and resurrection and exaltation mediate salvation to us and sustain that salvation. He is always interceding for us. His work is an eternal prayer to God on our behalf, and if the prayer of a righteous person is very powerful (James 5:16), then the prayer of Jesus, the very righteousness of God incarnate in man, is all-powerful. And this prayer is made on our behalf.

But wait, it gets better.

Can't think of what to pray, how to pray, when to pray, or what to pray *for*? The Holy Spirit has you covered, just as the Son does. Paul writes:

> Likewise the Spirit helps us in our weakness. For we do not know what to pray for as we ought, but the Spirit himself intercedes for us with groanings too deep for words. (Rom. 8:26)

There is no cause for frustration, guilt, or shame in prayer. The good news is that our Father loves us and knows our weaknesses. He sees our hearts, whether they are inclined to him or not. And the gospel tells us that Christ died for hearts not inclined toward him. Now that we are reconciled to the Father, despite our sin and stupidity, the Son and the Spirit pray for us even still, pleading the blood of Christ on our behalf for all time.

The gospel of prayer is that we need not pray to earn favor with God but rather to enjoy God's favor already given to us in Jesus. And the good news about prayer is that this favor is applied by the Trinity praying *within itself* about and for us. Isn't that amazing?

Becoming Friends with Jesus

My friend Ray is the most Jesusy guy I know. Half of him seems to exist in the spiritual ether at all times. He simultaneously radiates a warmth, a gentleness, a sweetness, and an incredible strength. He reminds me of what Jesus in person must be like.

Once upon a time, when Ray and I pastored churches in the same city, we started a group for pastors to gather and share stories and be encouraged by the gospel. One day there were about four of us in Ray's study, and Ray suddenly said, "Let me tell you about my friend Jesus." And he started telling us about Jesus, and it became very clear that Ray *actually knows Jesus*. Like, he actually hangs out with him.

And as Ray started describing his friend Jesus to us, the room changed. It got smaller and bigger at the same time. The air seemed to get sweeter, more breathable. I can't rightly say what happened, but my friend David, who was also there, confirmed he'd had the same experience. All I could figure was that we were somehow encountering a deeper sense of the presence of Jesus Christ, all because our Jesusy friend Ray was introducing us to him.

I want to be Jesusy like that. In my heart of hearts, I don't care about being seen as a big deal, about having a lot of recognition or a lot of stuff or even a lot of "spiritual experiences."

What I want is to truly know Jesus, to be actual friends with Jesus. And I know Ray would not say he got that way by happenstance. I know he'd say he got that way by God's grace, by the power of the Spirit. But I know Ray experienced that grace and power by listening to God and spilling his guts. He'd gotten off the treadmill of routine religion and found the rhythms of the kingdom. And it made him good friends with Jesus.

6

The Revolution Will Not Be Instagrammed

(When You Think Church Would Be Better without All the People)

> The Bible knows nothing
> of solitary religion.
>
> A "serious man"
> to John Wesley[1]

My gospel has been both a welcome mat and a place mat. It is a little messy. Scrape it with your fingernail and you'll disturb the crust of dusty footprints and dribbles of spaghetti sauce. This gospel gets passed around a lot. It's been under a lot of noses, in front of a lot of eyes. We've held hands around it, held it together before our faces like a shared song sheet at a Sunday night hymn sing, perhaps even wiped our tears with it. This gospel has all of our DNA on it, I'm afraid.

Dietrich Bonhoeffer once said that we meet one another as bringers of the gospel.[2] There's really no other point to getting together the way we do. Oh, sure, some churches are specializing in the individual experience, but the natural trajectory of that is simply staying at home. The acoustics are sometimes better and you don't have to put on clothes.

No, we don't gather to enjoy our individuality in the same room; we meet each other as bringers of the gospel. The gospel is designed to be *said*—it's not just a good idea; it's good news.

I know why many Christians avoid getting too involved in their churches or sometimes avoid church altogether. When I was a very young man trying to figure out what it meant to pursue a call into vocational ministry, I found myself in a very painful church experience. I was desperate for a mentor, but the men in leadership around me seemed downright hostile. I could not figure out what I had done wrong, and I couldn't get a meeting with any of them to ask how I'd offended them. Instead, I lived every ministry day in the middle of a bizarre kind of psychological warfare. It was about enough to make me give up the idea of ministry altogether.

I was young, green, and vulnerable. And I got chewed up and spit out. *If this is what church behind the public curtain of Sunday mornings is actually like*, I thought, *I don't want to have anything to do with it.*

But it was church that rescued me from church. My wife and I eventually defected, as difficult as it was, and found ourselves on the team of a new church plant where we found not only ministry roles that helped us grow in our gifts but also a community that helped us flourish in our faith. We could be honest about our sins and our struggles and we didn't find those confessions exploited. There was no ministerial spirit of competition or lusts for power strangling our own ambitions to follow Jesus on mission. We found a safe place to be sinners. We saw what judgment does to the honest and it was very, very bitter. Then we tasted what grace does to the honest, and it was very, very sweet.

The church has got to be a place where it's okay to not be okay.

But we have to be careful that our avoidance of Christian community in the local church is not the result of our own judgmental spirit. Too many believers wind up as just new, self-involved versions of the Pharisee looking down his nose at the tax collector (Luke 18:11), only this time they are outside the temple, sneering at the ones filing in: "I thank you, God, that I'm not like those fake churchgoing Christians!"

Up to this point, we've been mainly looking at the individual considerations of followship of Jesus. This makes sense as a beginning, because we each have to own our faith—it can't be inherited. Our faith, like our sins, is personal. But this doesn't mean that our faith ought to be private.

The danger we face in identifying our idols, pursuing Jesus through his gospel, and engaging in spiritual disciplines is that we end up treating Christianity like some kind of self-improvement routine. I hope by this point I've adequately demonstrated that such a focus is flatly antithetical to Christianity!

The gospel is a family meal. It is meant to be enjoyed regularly and intentionally in the presence of others and for the benefit of others.

Somehow, inside, we know this. We are wired for community, actually, even those of us who are sometimes painfully introverted. Even in our self-interest we demonstrate our underlying relational impulse.

Faux Community

Suburban Christians like to think they are good at community. From the PTA to the public parks, we play at this illusion constantly. The most visible example of the illusion of community in our consumer culture is the coffee shop. Coffee shops are often set up to look like a living room. Starbucks, for instance, provides couches and loveseats and sometimes even supplies board games. Most of them are trying to recapture the presence of the "third place" in American culture. A third place is a place where people go that is not work or home. Third places are places where people gather, apart from obligation, in order to experience community.

But what the coffee shops (and the cafés, and probably even the bars these days) have actually provided is a place for neighbors to come to be alone together. When I go to a coffee shop, it is usually to work or relax by myself, and I am usually surrounded by other lonesome souls with headphones in their ears and laptops in their faces. We all do our best not to bother each other.

The architecture and infrastructure of suburbia itself reflect the shift in our culture from actual community to the illusion. Most suburban homes are in close proximity to each other, in neighborhoods with a high density of houses. But looking more closely reveals the shift that has taken place in our posture toward our neighbors. Once upon a time, the front porch was the place to be. You sat outside and greeted those who passed. You knew your neighbors—or at least knew their names—and community life was the fabric of social success. But today's suburban homes are pushed way back from the street. And the "sitting out" activity has moved from the front porch to the back deck. Even the design of the homes themselves has changed, with the most livable rooms pushed to the rear of houses, separated by foyers and hallways and dens we rarely actually use. We now live in the day of privacy fences. Reflecting on this situation, author Skye Jethani surmises, "Everything about suburban home design communicates to the passerby, 'Leave me alone!'"[3]

All of this environmental insulation, in the midst of close proximity to others we basically ignore while we rub shoulders with them, creates a dysfunction in us about the idea of community and the gospel of reconciliation. It has severe ramifications in church life.

And so does the ever-morphing phenomenon of social media. It seems strange now to talk about social media in this way, as if it is something people do, something people "go on." (Remember when we had to "go onto" the internet? You heard a dial tone and a series of buzzy pings, like your computer was conducting a underwater search for your email using sonar.) Now, nobody "gets onto" the internet. We're always on. The internet has become the very matrix of life and culture itself. We carry constant connectivity in our pockets. The web has become the atmosphere.

And yet, as the virtual world becomes less virtual, as our near-ubiquitous connectivity has shrunk the globe, we are not any less isolated. And we aren't any more real. Even our transparency, our "authenticity," is a posture. We show what we want to show.

I think, for instance, of the social platform Instagram. Apparently everybody lives in a golden field, in a renovated farmhouse whitewashed with organic paint and decorated with bowls of ripe fruit positioned just so. The children all wear adorable galoshes, the men flannel, the women paisley sundresses they have made themselves from fabric bought down at the ol' mercantile "in town." When they're not taking pictures of their permanently vintage-filter family (#blessed), they are posting inspirational quote graphics. The whole thing is brilliant and lovely and heartwarming and cute as a button.

It's also fakey fake-fake. It's a ruse. Ninety-eight percent of family life is simply Not Ready for Instagram.

Is it any wonder so many of us struggle with church community? Because it doesn't seem Instagram-worthy, like, *ever*. You put a bunch of people together who aren't even blood related and expect them to be as utterly devoted to each other as blood relatives ought to be? You ask them to open up to each other? To share with each other the reality beneath the social media shams we're all so busy perpetrating?

Why would we do this?

Well, maybe because there isn't any other legitimate option. The life of Christian discipleship is designed to be lived in community, and if you get beyond those awesome couple of verses about "The Fellowship of the Believers" in Acts 2, you see that even in its earliest forms, the early church was not Instagrammable.

But it turned the world upside down.

The old covenant was made with God's chosen people, and the new covenant is made with God's called-out people. Jesus began his ministry with twelve friends and assorted other hangers-on. The book of Acts details the birth of the church as it did life together. The rest of the New Testament is written to church communities.

As Paul says at one point, one part of a body cannot say to another, "I don't need you!" (see 1 Cor. 12:21).

The way we lead our life—even our spiritual life—is like effectively placing a big "Do Not Disturb" sign over our life. But those of us who know anything about the way of Jesus know he ignores all such signs. He doesn't care one iota about your personal space. He knows—and we should admit—that our faux community desperately needs to be disturbed.

He even ought to come disturb our precious little mega-churchianity too. Because a self-esteem project masquerading as discipleship has infected the way we "do church," and our religious institutions are not immune to the fig leaves of faux community.

The very presence of the church should be a constant, living proclamation, like a lighthouse, of the benefits and blessings of community. Today this *must* mean embodying the biblically prescribed counterculture of the kingdom, challenging everyone who lives in the world to not live as those who are *of* it. Instead, our churches often reflect and emulate their cultures rather than challenge them. We have opted for being a mirror rather than a light.

Abandoning the reflection of culture and adopting the challenge (and caretaking) of culture will require our churches to think of their ministries less and less as a place where religious goods and services are provided and more and more as a training center where the community is inspired and empowered by the regular preaching of the gospel to follow Jesus, and where it learns how to serve its neighbors and each other in his name.

The business of a local church as a provider of spiritual goods and services to Christian consumers is pervasive and difficult to counteract, because in our hearts we are essentially consumers. Because our culture both feeds our consumption and stirs up more desires for consumption within us, a church that appeals to our passivity, that reflects our susceptibility to shiny things, appetites, and pride, can sometimes be the most appealing option. Churches that require little more than spectatorship but supply a vast array of programs, classes, and services do extremely well in our consumer culture. Many of us choose church communities not because of brother-hood or relational connection or submission to the idea of community itself but rather because the music is better, the services are at more convenient times, the youth ministry is well-resourced, or some other appealing feature.

The result of all this is the customer-driven church, where everything is tailored and marketed directly for maximum impact among maximum crowds. In the customer-driven church, the churchgoer is in the seat of honor. The customer, as they say, is always right. The problem with this is that the entry point for the kingdom is the denial and crucifixion of self.

Another problem is that every church hosts multiple cus-tomers. When we're all there for ourselves, not only do we not reap the best benefits of Christian discipleship but we're barely even a church. There is no concept of the church in the New Testament as a collection of individuals with individual ambitions and preferences. The whole enterprise is driven from the outside by the Spirit of God and mechanized on the inside by the unity of community.

Even when it comes to community efforts by churches, the way is rough going. The dirty little secret of modern church programming is that small group programs are not working well.[4] We all recognize they are key to cultivating the need for community in our churches, but most of us also recognize they are notoriously difficult to pull off. There are a lot of reasons for this, but they all boil down primarily to the fact that American Christians don't want to experience community. Or, at least, they want other things *more*.

At the outset of creation, God looked at solitary Adam and announced that it was not good for man to be alone. But in the day of the customer-driven church, we basically respond, "Nah, it'll be okay."

But we are not okay.

The Rhythms Are for Community

The amazing thing about the gospel is that it creates reconciliation not just between humanity and God but also between people. We see the original division between humankind through the fall of Adam and Eve in the book of Genesis. A part of the curse of their disobedience is relational conflict between each other, and this sets up the dilemma of self-centered division from our neighbor, first most vividly illustrated when Cain pooh-poohs the idea that he might be Abel's keeper.

We also see this division reflected in the Ten Commandments. The first four commandments correspond to our division from God, our vertical relationship. The last six correspond to our division from others, our horizontal relationships. And Jesus reflects this division as well in the Great Commandment, when he connects loving God with loving our neighbor.

Because the division caused by sin is an all-encompassing division—cutting us off from God and, therefore, from each other—the gospel is an all-encompassing remedy. Jesus's atoning work reconciles us to God but it also reconciles us to each other. Or, rather, it *should*. The gospel creates the culture of reconciliation, which the New Testament calls the church.

Peter elaborates on the nature of the church this way:

> But you are a chosen race, a royal priesthood, a holy nation, a people for his own possession, that you may proclaim the excellencies of him who called you out of darkness into his marvelous light. Once you were not a people, but now you are God's people. (1 Pet. 2:9–10)

What do all of Peter's descriptors for the church have in common? They are collective nouns. Race. Priesthood. Nation. People. These concepts cannot be manifested individually.

Many of us are familiar with the powerful picture of Christian community and the ideal portrait of church ministry in Acts 2. Luke's description of the church's activity in verses 42–47 has become the goal of many churches in their desire to cultivate community. But two chapters later, Luke reiterates the miraculous ministry of the church in a more expansive and illustrative way. Right after Peter and John are released from Sanhedrin custody,

> they went to their friends and reported what the chief priests and the elders had said to them. And when they heard it, they lifted their voices together to God and said, "Sovereign Lord, who made the heaven and the earth and the sea and everything in them, who through the mouth of our father David, your servant, said by the Holy Spirit,

> "'Why did the Gentiles rage,
>   and the peoples plot in vain?
> The kings of the earth set themselves,
>   and the rulers were gathered together,
>   against the Lord and against his Anointed—'

for truly in this city there were gathered together against your holy servant Jesus, whom you anointed, both Herod and Pontius Pilate, along with the Gentiles and the peoples of Israel, to do whatever your hand and your plan had predestined to take place. And now, Lord, look upon their threats and grant to your servants to continue to speak your word with all boldness, while you stretch out your hand to heal, and signs and wonders are performed through the name of your holy Servant Jesus." And when they had prayed, the place in which they were gathered together was shaken, and they were all filled with the Holy Spirit and continued to speak the word of God with boldness.

Now the full number of those who believed were of one heart and soul, and no one said that any of the things that belonged to him was his own, but they had everything in common. And with great power the apostles were giving their testimony to the resurrection of the Lord Jesus, and great grace was upon them all. There was not a needy person among them, for as many as were owners of lands or houses sold them and brought the proceeds of what was sold and laid it at the apostles' feet, and it was distributed to each as any had need. (Acts 4:23–35)

The first thing we notice about this passage is that Peter and John return to their church family and report that the Sanhedrin has warned them not to continue preaching the gospel and that doing so could cost them greatly, perhaps even their lives. The response of the church is amazing. They do not despair. They respond in praise and prayer. Their prayer is so stirring, the building shakes with the presence of the Spirit.

What we see in Acts 4 is the full concert of the rhythms of the kingdom in their proper context: the Christian community. The Acts 4 church listens to and feels Scripture together, prays together, joyfully fasts together, and serves others together. Today's church should do no less.

The mistake we may make is using a book like this to seek spiritual exercises for our personal journey. But none of the kingdom rhythms can be sustained independently. The gospel presupposes and prescribes reconciliation; it announces salvation for individuals and a community of salvation. *We need each other.* The Christian life must be walked within the encouragement, edification, and accountability of Christian community. We need teachers to teach us how to do it, encouragers to inspire and sustain us, givers to remind us to give, helpers to help us embrace servitude, prophets to speak truth to us, and so forth.

To abide in Christ necessitates embracing the body of Christ as God's plan for the Christian life. Abiding in Christ can't be experienced as it's designed to be experienced apart from abiding in the community called his very body. And the further good news is that embracing kingdom rhythms becomes easier and more sustainable when it is done alongside others.

The community called the church, then, moving according to the rhythms of the kingdom, is like a great big dance.

But if you're like me you hate dances—great big ones, especially. If you're like me, you approach the dance as one who wants to look like he belongs there without really participating too much. You want to stand against the wall, bobbing your head to the music while not actually getting onto the floor. Because then you'd look like an idiot.

And a lot of people try to do church like that. Just enough involvement to not get hassled about not being involved but not enough involvement to actually be involved. A lot of disciples flit around on the periphery of church life, showing up when it's comfortable, pitching in when it's convenient, speaking up only when we stand to lose something. Steve Timmis and Tim Chester say that most Christians love the idea of community—until it begins to infringe upon their decision making.[5]

And then we wonder why our walk with Christ never really seems to take off. We treat the church the way we hope Jesus never treats us, keeping us at arm's length because we're weird or messy or socially awkward. But if the holy God of the universe affectionately welcomes all those losers to himself, who do we think we are when we refuse to do so ourselves? Paul says, "Welcome one another as Christ has welcomed you" (Rom. 15:7). But until we engage fully in the messy community of discipleship, we cannot expect to feel Christ fully engaged in the mess of us.

In fact, these two primary Spiritual rhythms we've already looked at—listening to God in his Word and speaking to God in prayer—take us to new depths of understanding and new heights of holiness when we practice them together.

Listening to Scripture in Community

How would you know if your theology sucked?

Many of us have learned how rewarding studying the Bible with other believers can be. Studying Scripture with others will take us places in the Bible we may not venture on our own. This, too, enhances our ability to feel Scripture.

It's no surprise that people bring different perspectives, insights, experiences, and educations to their study of the Bible, and when we study together we get the benefit of a multifaceted, greater-dimensioned look at the Word. We may be able to read more at once when we're studying alone, but we likely miss more than we cover. Studying the Bible for one's self is imperative for the growing Christian, but studying the Bible with others is even more so.

Yes, it can be awkward and sluggish. Sometimes people ask weird questions or make dumb statements. (It's especially awkward when that person is you.) But sometimes people ask questions we haven't considered, reveal insights we haven't anticipated. And what good is our own biblical knowledge if it is only hoarded up in our private study, never used to build up or encourage others? Don't be a miser with your Bible.

When we withdraw from the life of Christian community and try to practice the kingdom rhythms alone, we actually quench the Spirit who gifts the church to follow Jesus as a body and defy Jesus's prayer that we all be one.

In addition, removing ourselves from communal study of the Bible is a way of saying our ears work best, that nobody else hears as well as we do. And yet God has gifted some Christians to be teachers. If he has gifted some to teach, why would we not want to learn from those the Lord himself has gifted? And even if we happen to be gifted to teach, we still need to experience the teaching of others. What we see in the snapshots of the early church in the New Testament is the called-out community devoting themselves to the teaching of the apostles together. In Acts 4, they are praying "unanimously" using the Old Testament. In other depictions we see them learning together and discussing. In still others they gather and listen to preaching. There is "iron sharpening iron" at work in these gatherings (see Prov. 27:17).

From the larger gathering of worship services to the gathering of small groups, the blueprint for Bible study in the early church was a team event. Perhaps the best way to cultivate a feeling for Scripture is experiencing bold preaching and devoted community groups. As we study Scripture together, we begin to interpret it through a communal lens and ponder its implications not just for our individual life but for our church.

Prayer in Community

Maybe your church excels at this, but it's become pretty routine for a church to ensure low attendance by scheduling a prayer service. Pastors, the first thing you ought to do about your people's reluctance to pray is *pray*. Pray for them. And with them. And by them and in front of them.

A few years ago I spoke to a representative from a parachurch organization who spent many Sundays in our area visiting local churches to network and talk about his ministry. He remarked on the amount of prayer in our worship service, saying that in his travels he found it rare that a church would devote so much time to corporate prayer during service. We prayed here and there throughout the service and even had an extended time we called "Prayer and Share," where congregants could voice requests or testimonies.

But lest I sound like I'm really trumpeting the prayerful devotion of my ministry, I should mention that whenever our leaders internally discussed strategically shortening our worship service—for the sake of visiting unbelievers, for example—the extended prayer time was usually the first point of evaluation. We all had to constantly fight against the temptation to find prayer expendable.

None of us is ever in danger of praying too much.

From corporate prayer in worship services to shared prayer in small groups, we learn to pray by learning to pray together. There can be no more intimate moment with our brothers and sisters in Christ than approaching together the throne room of God through Christ and in the Spirit. In communal prayer we reveal the desires and depressions of our heart. We reveal what matters most to us. We share our burdens. We connect to each other as we connect to God.

One of the key ways relational intimacy develops in times of shared prayer is through confession. The first thing we ought to confess is our sin of not confessing our sins to each other. James writes, "Therefore, confess your sins to one another and pray for one another, so that you may be healed" (5:16). Is there anything more frequently left out of group prayer than confession? I believe our reluctance and fear to confess our sins to each other is a direct result of our failure to cultivate authentic community in our churches. The two feed each other: confession creates communal intimacy, and communal intimacy produces confession. When we confess our sins to each other, we set up the opportunity to share the gospel with each other, and there's no greater privilege God gives us than to share the good news.

Another aspect of communal prayer that is actually a required work of the church community is the celebration of

Communion. Whether we are eating the Lord's Supper in a small group or in a worship service, the family meal of Christ's body and blood is the most powerful and Christ-exalting way to proclaim the gospel to each other and our collective allegiance to God. The commemoration of the Lord's Supper is a prayer of confession—"Because I am a sinner, I need the body and blood of Christ to live"—and a prayer of commitment—"We believe in and subsist on Christ alone for forgiveness, righteousness, and power." That the Lord's Supper is a family meal, meant to be eaten with our brothers and sisters in an act of worship, makes it the most profound prayer of all.

Would You Join a Club That Would Have You as a Member?

When we can get over the fact that the church isn't Instagram-ready, something amazing happens. First of all, this is what grace is for! We don't need grace at the Instagrammable church.

But at the real church? The one with the snot-nosed kids and the cantankerous old folks and the arrogant hipsters and the out-of-touch baby boomers and the pastor with his short-sleeved button-up shirt tucked into his high-waisted Dockers and the overweight "praise team"? Well, that's the kind of place where grace can really show off. Grace is pronouncedly stronger in churches profoundly weak.

I mean, do you think *you're* hot stuff? If you're hot stuff, stop reading this book. It's not for winners.

No, the actual church isn't the church in the stock photos. (Not sure what those guys raising their hands out in the middle of wheat fields are doing but I'm fairly certain it does not resemble what takes place in your worship service.) The actual church is a motley crew of sinners who are more primed, together, to really experience grace than they would be if they were all apart.

And when grace takes over a church? When grace changes the conversation? When we stop sucking in our guts, stop with the religious preening, and stop hanging around the margins, tapping our foot with our back to the wall? When we take a chance, get out and dance our dorky dance, and risk looking stupid in front of each other in order to finally, at long last, be ourselves?

Okay, sometimes we'll get laughed at. Sometimes it goes badly. I'm not going to lie to you. It doesn't always go so well. If you've been a follower of Jesus for any significant length of time, you probably have some experience of finding your risk-taking for grace landing you right on your face.

But it's worth taking that risk because many times our honesty and transparency liberate others from their own prisons of "having it all together." Our courage to be failures gives permission to others to "own up," and when we all own up together, the Lord does not punish us. He rewards us! A community that is willing to get honest about its sins and its weaknesses and its brokenness finds the abundance of grace it has been longing for.

Grace does this to a church that is desperate for it. There is a sweetness, a palpable kindness, a gentleness that begins to override the previous pretense, the Instagrammable illusions none of us can keep up for long in close relationships anyway. Paul prays this beautiful prayer for the church: "May the God of endurance and encouragement grant you to live in such harmony with one another, in accord with Christ Jesus" (Rom. 15:5).

The church Paul is writing to is experiencing a unity of doctrine, sure. But it is also experiencing the harmony of what that doctrine produces. The doctrine of grace when administered with a spirit of grace gradually becomes a culture of grace.

A message of grace will attract people but a culture of grace will *keep* them.

See, the gospel cannot make us into little judges of each other's ministerial output. It cannot make us people who keep sizing each other up, measuring each other, rehearsing each other's failings. It's not tuned to the frequency of accusation. We instead become *advocates* for our brothers and sisters.

If anything, we should be astounded they let us into the community. Given what we know of ourselves, given that we are the worst sinners we know, it is a staggeringly arrogant thing to begrudge any other repentant follower of Jesus a place at the dance. If the bar was low enough to allow our entry, what advantage is there to raising it?

The gospel requires self-denial; applying the gospel to our community means bearing with the failings of the weak, not trying to please ourselves first, and pleasing our neighbors for their good, to build them up (vv. 1–2).

The gospel cannot puff us up; it cannot make us prideful; it cannot make us selfish; it cannot make us arrogant; it cannot make us rude; it cannot make us gossipy; it cannot make us accusers. So it stands to reason that the more we press into the gospel, the more the gospel takes over our hearts and the spaces we bring our hearts to, the less we would see those things.

You cannot grow in holiness and holier-than-thou-ness at the same time.

Now, this scares people who believe God has delegated his sovereignty to them. But it honors the gospel of Jesus, in whom there is no condemnation and through whom we are being built together—as we welcome each other—as a place of welcome for the Spirit of the living God. In the kingdom to which the church is meant to bear witness, people flourish and become at the same time more like their real selves and more like Jesus Christ.

So this means that, instead of coming to church with our preferences, we seek first our real priorities. Instead of coming with a desire for our own fulfillment, we seek the flourishing of others.

We seek out the covenant of church membership, then, not simply for its privileges but for its responsibilities and obligations. We want not to join the club, in other words, but rather to join *the mission*.

And this means approaching the community of faith not as a consumer but as a contributor. It means, if I can use this language—and it's my book, so I say I can—becoming a "low-maintenance" church member.

Is Your Pastor Happy to See You?

I wish that when I was a pastor I had spent more time with all the low-maintenance church folks. In church life, the squeaky wheel, as they say, gets the grease. Meanwhile, the folks who quietly and humbly serve, give, and simply show up without causing heartaches or headaches just keep on keepin' on. God love 'em. I sure did. They were a joy to me, and I fear I neglected them simply because they didn't seem too needy.

It is my goal now, for as long as God would have me simply as a sheep and not a shepherd, to be as low-maintenance as I can manage for my church. When my pastor sees me coming—his name is Nathan (Hi, Nathan, if you're reading this)—I want him not to inwardly sigh or tense up or have to marshal some extra patience or energy but to relax a little, smile, and feel safe.

As a twenty-plus-year veteran of ministry who knows an awful lot of pastors, I can tell you that this feeling can be rare. There's even a Bible verse about this, and it's one that many pastors are too scared to ever preach on. I'm going to do them all a favor right now and share it with you:

> Obey your leaders and submit to them, for they are keeping watch over your souls, as those who will have to give an account. Let them do this with joy and not with groaning, for that would be of no advantage to you. (Heb. 13:17)

Some of you reading this might actually need to print that out and tape it to your mirror or the dashboard of your car.

Yes, there are some bad pastors out there. There are some authoritarian, domineering leaders out there. Too many, in fact. Some pastors are indeed bullies. These people need to be held accountable and in many cases removed from their position of authority, as the biblical qualifications for the pastoral office forbid the quarrelsome, short-tempered, domineering person any part in church leadership.

But can I be honest? In my forty years in the church, despite some negative experiences with a few pastors, I've encountered way more bullies in the pews than in the pulpits. There are just as many pastors victimized by graceless congregants as vice versa.

I have a pastor friend who said he once dared to preach on Hebrews 13:17 and had no sooner read the verse at the start of his message—hadn't even started preaching yet!—when a woman stood up and shouted, "We're Baptist. We don't submit to anybody!"

You may not be Baptist, but you do need to submit to your church leaders. The Bible says so. Argue with it, if you want, but know that you are arguing with God.

To be a Christian is to be a churchman or churchwoman. As I've said, the New Testament knows of no vibrant discipleship apart from life in the local church and no authentic Christianity divorced from the covenant of life together according to the biblical structure of the local church. And if this is true, it behooves us to be the best undamned churchman or churchwoman we can be. And good church folks love, respect, and submit to their pastors.

This does not mean idolizing them, treating them like celebrities, or becoming yes-men. It doesn't mean becoming our pastor's rubber stamp committee. But it does mean giving grace not just to your fellow sheep but also to your shepherds. In fact, they may need more, as the responsibilities they carry are more burdensome and they will have to give a greater account before God. Submitting to your leaders means repenting of the impulse to "yes, but" everything they say, especially if what they say isn't sinful. In matters of differences of opinion, it means being circumspect in how we voice our own. It means remembering that playing the "devil's advocate" is not a good thing. The devil doesn't need any advocates in the church!

Generally speaking, submitting to your elders means maintaining a posture of encouragement and gracious support for them and working to make the church a safe place for them (and their families!). Some people in our churches see it as their role to "keep the pastor honest." These people are usually the kind that make the pastors keeping watch over them groan.

Look, you may be a total mess. You may have a lot of pain and a lot of struggle. You may find it frustrating to get your act together. If you know this about yourself, why not give the same grace to your leaders that you expect for yourself?

And if you think it should be a great honor to your leaders to get to shepherd you, you're probably the most groan-worthy of all. It's the ones who reckon themselves as being totally put together who usually cause the biggest problems.

How can we work toward our leaders' joy and not their anxiety? It's no advantage to us to be a nagging pain to our pastors. They will have to give an account for how they pastored us. And we'll have to give an account for how well we presented ourselves to be pastored.

Congregations Have Wish Dreams Too

In my favorite book on the life of the church, *Life Together*, Dietrich Bonhoeffer writes:

> When a person becomes alienated from a Christian community in which he has been placed and begins to raise complaints about it, he had better examine himself first to see whether the trouble is not due to his wish dream that should be shattered by God.[6]

As a pastor, I took the particular section on what Bonhoeffer calls the "wish dream" very much to heart. I wrote extensively on this subject in a book on pastoral ministry,[7] but the gist was this: the vision for the church that a pastor wants can get in the way of their ministry to the church God has actually given them, and because the wish dream church is an idol, it prevents them from actually loving their church well.

I think Bonhoeffer's words are quite sobering and every pastor ought to consider them well. Idolatry is never far from us. From *any* of us.

Because church folks have wish dreams too. They can have a wish-dream church experience or community. They can have wish-dream pastors. And these visions quench the Spirit's working in the real stuff of church and ministry.

When a congregation becomes preoccupied with a vision for the church experience it wants and then has to actually participate in the messiness of authentic Christian community, the contrast is jarring. I have pastored congregant after congregant who found me and the church community itself handy scapegoats for their marriage problems, their depression problems, their socialization problems, and on and on. Disappointed by the church's failure to measure up to their expectations and ideals, they began to complain and the justifications of their complaints took root, along with bitterness and irritation.

When a church person becomes preoccupied with their vision of the ideal pastor, their current pastor's flaws become more pronounced, more egregious. Scores are kept. Misunderstandings and misinterpretations flourish. Slights are imagined. Strengths seem negligible, weaknesses insurmountable. The criticism begins, then the grapevine chatter, the anonymous complaints, the cold shoulders, the specious charges, the spirit of discouragement. All of it gets spiritualized, even as the wish dreamer's heart is hardening. The wish dream keeps churches from loving their pastors and often abets hurting them.

This happens among longtime churchgoers and new believers alike. New believers especially may be at risk of judgmental wish dreaming, because it is deceptively easy to move from enthusiasm and zeal of new faith to wondering why everybody else isn't as enthusiastic and zealous as they are. They start measuring, comparing. Their focus subtly shifts from the Lord's standard of holiness to their own excitement. We can all fall into this rut because we're all basically spiritual screwups.

Too many church folks are expecting their pastors or their churches to complete them, to virtually "be Jesus" to them. But only Jesus can be Jesus to us. There's only one Messiah. So if we're expecting all our inner dysfunction and awkwardness and hurts and fears to get fixed by the experience of Christian community, good luck with that. Everybody else is expecting the same thing. We're a bunch of beggars demanding the other beggars give them bread.

Ask yourself: How do you see people? Truly.

The different personalities and personal idiosyncrasies that make Christian community so vibrant also make it fraught with relational peril. Extroverts sometimes use the community to give the illusion of relational intimacy when really they're just using people. Introverts often distance themselves from Christian community, retreating into the alleged safety of their solitude, effectively saying, "I have no need of you." Bonhoeffer says about this dual dynamic: "Let him who cannot be alone beware of community. Let him who is not in community beware of being alone."[8]

Maybe you think church would be great if it weren't for the people. But if it weren't for the people, you would not know the depths of the gospel the way Jesus wants you to. Maybe it's time your wish dream gets shattered. You're not all you're cracked up to be either, you know.

What We Are Together

The brilliant, God-designed blueprint for kingdom life in Jesus's Sermon on the Mount envisions a community called by God, formed by God, and led by God into worship and outward mission that draws a lost world to behold the glory of God. When we as a community of Christ-followers demonstrate our life in Christ together through our feeling of Scripture, our prayer, our fasting, our service, and our relational intimacy, we create a compelling announcement of the kingdom's presence in the world. This compelling announcement is what Jesus refers to when he says:

> You are the salt of the earth, but if salt has lost its taste, how shall its saltiness be restored? It is no longer good for anything except to be thrown out and trampled under people's feet.
> You are the light of the world. A city set on a hill cannot be hidden. Nor do people light a lamp and put it under a basket, but on a stand, and it gives light to all in the house. In the same way, let your light shine before others, so that they may see your good works and give glory to your Father who is in heaven. (Matt. 5:13–16)

The "salt of the earth" Jesus talks about is not, strictly speaking, a reference to preservation, as you may have heard.

In Jesus's day, "salty speech" and the like referred to *flavor*. The idea Jesus is referencing is of the church adding "spice" to life, of being compelling in its message and mission. This is what Paul appeals to in Colossians 4:6 when he writes, "Let your speech always be gracious, seasoned with salt, so that you may know how you ought to answer each person." The church gives the compelling appeal of salt in the earth by making the good news sound and look good.

The other image Jesus offers in this passage is that of a city on a hill, a shining tower of hope set apart but illuminating all those around. The city on a hill image does not mean the church is to be distant from the world but rather visible to the world in the same way a shining light is in the darkness. The problem is that many churches today are very noticeable and very flashy—and their light shines on themselves. They broadcast their own greatness. But Jesus's aim for the church is the glory of God.

What we are talking about, when we get right down to it, is the difference between the customer-driven church and the missional church. In an ideal world, the idea of a "missional church" would be redundant, because the church by definition is supposed to be missional.

The two great failures of the evangelical church today are failures of the highest magnitude: neglecting to proclaim the gospel and refusing to embody it.

In 1 Corinthians 15:3–4 Paul defines the gospel as "of first importance." There is nothing more important than the good news that Jesus Christ died for sinners and rose again. This gospel is the primary message of the kingdom and the primary catalyst of the kingdom's spread. The gospel is power.

And yet consumer Christianity has essentially relegated it to the backseat of message and mission.

We ought to take great care that we do not unintentionally perpetuate the errors of preaching a gospel we do not embody or embodying a gospel we do not preach. Neither error is truly gospel. Both are attempts at talking about a rhythm without charting or playing it.

We must embrace both gospel-driven proclamation (light) and gospel-driven servanthood (salt), for both are vital to the ministry of reconciliation. The call to salt and light is a call to a two-fisted gospel, a call to crucify the idols of self and comfort and convenience and relevance and give ourselves away. Think of the brightness such light would have. The gospel is power and must be wielded with a whole heart.

The two-fisted gospel supposes one fist is to take out the prince of the power of the air with the revolutionary news that the risen Christ is Lord, and the second fist is to bring justice to the captives with the embodied news that God is love.

A loving force of that magnitude cannot be stopped. The gates of hell will not prevail against it. The God of peace will soon crush Satan under his feet. (Or fists!) A loving force of that magnitude will be unavoidably visible and undeniably compelling, like light and salt.

The rhythms of the kingdom, when played by the community called the church like a great biblical symphony, will sustain a worship song so powerful we will taste heaven and broadcast to others the all-surpassing glory of God.

Salt of the earth. Light of the world.

We are only these *together*. No Christian alone is the salt of the earth. No Christian is individually the light of the world. The church is the salt of the earth. The church is the light of the world.

I know the church can be very difficult to get into. And yet, as difficult and complex as messy discipleship is, it's incredibly easy to reproduce. "Crummy" discipleship is imminently replicable! Wherever people have to hear each other, see each other, and deal with each other in the context of God's glorious gospel, things will get messy. The good news is that messy is easy to replicate. So none of us is far from real discipleship. We don't have to be experts, just converts pointing each other to Jesus.

Finding the rhythm of community is frustrating sometimes. Some churches even forego it altogether and settle for some kind of experience they imagine to be a suitable replacement. Spirit becomes spectacle. A lot of energy goes into making the church as slick and glossy as we can. We spend a lot of money and commit a lot of gifts and talents and resources to making sure we don't have to see what grace might do with the lights on.

The real church isn't Instagrammable. But you can't dismiss it with a swipe. It endures forever. It may not look like much, but it's hellproof.

The un-messy church, on the other hand, might reek of perfection but it's far from ideal. It's "going with the times" and therefore going, as C. S. Lewis said, where all times go.

7 The Nine Irrefutable Laws of Followship

(When You Feel Stuck)

> To succeed in keeping the law one must
> aim at something other and something
> more. One must aim to become the *kind
> of person* from whom the deeds of the law
> naturally flow.
>
> Dallas Willard[1]

My gospel is burning a hole in my pocket. It's an ember smoldering, singeing my threads and my thigh. It is leaving a mark. It is branding me.

It cannot be contained. My gospel is a wildfire waiting to happen. It scorches dry earth, lays waste to dead limbs.

I think of the typical Christian Living section in the mainstream bookstore down at the suburban shopping center. Row after row of pseudo-religious gobbledygook promising breakthroughs and victories and super-colossal personal affirmations for abundant living. Jesus is quoted and appropriated in these shiny tomes, their glossy covers invariably featuring successful religious spokespersons grinning big-toothed grins under waves of well-coiffed hair. "Buy my millstone," their smiles say. "It's good for you."

My gospel wants to leap from my pocket and set fire to the whole damned bookcase.

Self-help doesn't help. My self is the problem. How can my self help my self?

Do you feel stuck? I very often do.

When I was responsible for preaching a sermon every week, I would often think about this feeling, this overwhelming sense of being stuck. I thought about the people who would file through the church doors on Sunday, many of them carrying enormous burdens—wounds from their pasts, the pressure of present anxieties, the shame of secret sins. And there were plenty of Sundays when I took to the pulpit just plain worn out. I had quickly tired of trying to give people some kind of cheerleading routine from the Bible. I rapidly realized that it takes some people all the faith they've got that week just to get through the church doors. And what was I going to do? Throw a bunch of "tools" at them? Tell them they have what it takes? They were there on Sunday morning because somehow, in their hearts, they knew that wasn't true! If any of us have what it takes, why are we going to church in the first place?

I also knew this feeling of stuck-ness had to inform the way I discipled and counseled and mentored. I needed to teach people to engage in the spiritual disciplines, but I had to do it in such a way that they could be sure God was at work in them. That no matter how stuck they felt, they'd know Jesus wasn't going to leave them behind, flailing for help from the quicksand of their own lame devotional times.

Look, the gospel has to be good news for the stuck too. Or else it's not good news.

But we so crave something else, something more. We crave the latest, greatest, newest, biggest advice. And we can find it often on our churchy bookshelves. There's an endless supply of self-help books every year for two primary reasons: not a single one of them works, but we keep believing they will. Our flesh yearns for salvation by works.

Christian radio host Brant Hansen has done a wonderful job of skewering the discipleship-industrial complex's infatuation with the kind of "Christian leadership" resources that go hand in hand with these self-help Christian Living books. He calls it:

The 417 Rules of Awesomely Bold Leadership

I've successfully taught awesomely bold leaders for years: When under pressure, under stress, you must breathe. You must inhale, then exhale, repeatedly.

How successful is it? Friends, as my wonderful, God fearing grandmother used to say, the proof is in the pudding! Patriots quarterback Tom Brady employs this "in-and-out" breathing method, as does NASCAR star Jimmie Johnson and the last five U.S. Presidents, except Ronald Reagan, who no longer employs this breathing method. What do they know that you don't?

I lack space here to explain it all. Suffice it to say, science is confirming what Awesomely Bold Leaders in my seminars already know: When we're under stress, our brains require oxygen.[2]

Yes and amen. But the dirty little secret about all these Five Steps to Awesome Living and Seven Tips for Conquering Your Fears and Nine Irresistible Levels of Maximum Potentialization is that they don't actually help us breathe better. They suffocate us.

Here's the deal: somewhere along the way, the Christian leadership culture decided that if we just made our laws more positive (more dos, as opposed to all the don'ts), we'd somehow make our teaching magically less legalistic. But "do" isn't any less legalistic than "don't." You may fashion it as more encouraging and helpful than burdensome and forbidding, but it's still a burden. Dos and don'ts accomplish nothing resembling biblical Christianity when they are detached from the *done* of the gospel. The gospel gives us oxygen and space to breathe.

It's a bizarre thing that happens in a lot of church services aimed at unbelievers. Worship service after worship service designed to make lost people more comfortable or more interested in Christianity offer them a steady diet of things to do while withholding from them the power with which to do it. Why would we expect "Christian living" from people who aren't born again? They aren't even spiritually alive.

Even after many of us are saved, we run ahead of the gospel into the field of the law, in our own power, trying to do great things for God or earn favor with him—all the while forgetting that the only thing the Bible calls *power* for obedience is the gospel and that it is actually *grace* that teaches us how to repent and obey.

In his letter to Titus, Paul paints a beautiful picture of the culture of discipleship inside a healthy church. In Titus

2:1–10, older men and women are demonstrating maturity in their followship of Jesus largely by passing on the faith to younger men and women who are maturing in their followship of Jesus. It's another great reminder that discipleship is not designed for the individual Christian life. Discipleship is meant to be experienced in the covenantal context of a Christian community.

As every Christian takes up the kingdom rhythms (Bible study, prayer, and so forth) within the harmonious life of the local church, we all become together more than we could be apart. We become together much more than what we could become following the chapters of the latest self-help book. We end up actually "adorn[ing] the doctrine of God our Savior" (Titus 2:10). And the wonderful thing is that, if we are actually Christians, this adornment is a foregone conclusion. We *will* be changed. Paul says in the midst of this impressive portrait of corporate followship of Jesus that it is grace that drives the whole thing (vv. 11–12).

You can't get away from this concept in the pages of Scripture. Biblically speaking, the power of our obedience and the source of our holiness is not our efforts but the finished work of Jesus Christ. It's God who works in us to will and to work (Phil. 2:12–13). Our good works were ordained beforehand (Eph. 2:10). The same gospel that empowers our conversion empowers our sanctification (Titus 2:11–12; 1 Cor. 15:1–2; Rom. 8:30). It is Jesus who both authors our faith and perfects it (Heb. 12:2). It is God alone who is faithful both to start the work in us and to complete it (Phil. 1:6).

It's not that we don't expend any energy. It is simply that the energy comes from God's Spirit (Col. 1:29). It's not we who are living but Christ who is living in us (Gal. 2:20).

This in itself is good news. If you're a Christian you will obey! The Spirit of God living inside of us ensures it. We will bear good fruit. This doesn't make us sinless. But it does make us sure of spiritual growth and it does make us more conscious of and convicted over our sin.

This gospel-driven way of living upends so much of the way many Christians "do" discipleship training. It's a curious thing that very often the gospel runs counter even to church cultures. And it certainly runs counter to the way of the world.

In Paul's letter to the Galatians, he uses up a lot of ink rebuking the church for giving a platform to heretics (the Judaizers) who have tried to piggyback legal burdens on the gospel. In insisting that circumcision, for example, was necessary for salvation, these false teachers essentially said, "Yes, grace, but . . ." And anytime you add a "but" to grace, you disgrace grace (Rom. 11:6). So Paul is heartbroken over the way the Galatians have opened themselves up to a bunch of butgraces.

As he develops his rebuke, he covers the biblical history of the covenant to show that he's not making this gospel stuff up. And then he wants to demonstrate that while the gospel is distinct from the law, it is not antithetical to the law. He is not implying that God is unconcerned about our obedience unto holiness. He just wants us to see that behavioral obedience is both worthless and pointless apart from a heart full of grace. Paul is helping us to understand that the kind of living that honors God best is the kind that comes by walking in the Spirit of the gospel. So he writes this:

> But I say, walk by the Spirit, and you will not gratify the desires of the flesh. For the desires of the flesh are against the Spirit, and the desires of the Spirit are against the flesh, for

these are opposed to each other, to keep you from doing the things you want to do. But if you are led by the Spirit, you are not under the law. Now the works of the flesh are evident: sexual immorality, impurity, sensuality, idolatry, sorcery, enmity, strife, jealousy, fits of anger, rivalries, dissensions, divisions, envy, drunkenness, orgies, and things like these. I warn you, as I warned you before, that those who do such things will not inherit the kingdom of God. But the fruit of the Spirit is love, joy, peace, patience, kindness, goodness, faithfulness, gentleness, self-control; against such things there is no law. And those who belong to Christ Jesus have crucified the flesh with its passions and desires. If we live by the Spirit, let us also keep in step with the Spirit. (Gal. 5:16–25)

In this passage Paul offers two corresponding lists: the works of the flesh and the fruit of the Spirit.

Notice that the first list, "desires of the flesh," runs the gamut of sinful behaviors, from drunkenness to jealousy and from sexual immorality to fits of anger. It includes things we tend to consider "big sins" and some things we tend to think aren't such a big deal. But there is really nothing left off this list, and there's no way of looking at this list and thinking your special sin has been left out. Paul even helpfully adds "and things like these" to tighten up any apparent loopholes.

Also notice this: the first list consists largely of actions, even if a few are more mental. The works of the flesh are more generally just that—works. This second list, though, the fruit of the Spirit, largely consists of what we might call *qualities* or conditions.

If we can take anything away from a blunt comparison of the lists, it might be this: the solution to bad things we do isn't good things to do but good things to *be*.

Look, I know religious people who don't have sex, don't get drunk, don't see R-rated movies, et cetera—but who are loveless, joyless, impatient, unkind, ungentle, et cetera.

So there we have the primary problem with so many approaches to Christian discipleship—they are predicated primarily on *doing* different rather than *becoming* different.

But because Paul calls these areas of growth the "fruit of the Spirit," he's showing us that these are things the Spirit produces. We aren't passive. But we aren't the prime mover. If we have repented of our sin and placed our faith in Jesus Christ—decisions also empowered by the Holy Spirit—the Holy Spirit is obliged to bear the fruit of these things in our life.

Now we've got an entirely new way of looking at the law, at God's commands and expectations. We are set free from the condemnation of the law to the spirit of the law. The Spirit is determined that we become holy. In this way, "Be holy, because I am holy" (1 Pet. 1:16 NIV) is not just a command but also a promise. We are gifted the holiness into which we have been called.

So, then, I offer a few irrefutable laws of my own. Or, rather, they aren't my laws. They are God's laws. And also his promises. These are based on the nine named "fruit" produced by the Spirit, according to Galatians 5:22–23.

1. Be Ye Loving

You don't have to be a Christian to believe that everybody should love everybody. We are bombarded by this message every day in a million different ways, from the plaintive pleadings of social justice warriors in the evening news to the sappy moralism broadcast by pop radio stations. And yet we are all lousy at this. None of us, left to our own devices and centered on our own fulfillment and happiness, can muster up the energy to love the way we think we ought to. More often than not, we are more concerned about people's love for us than we are our love for people.

Only the gospel orients our love appropriately, because only the gospel reminds us that we are more sinful than we realize (humbling us to see that, apart from Christ, we are just as needy as anybody else and thus have no justification for self-interest) and that we are more loved than we know (empowering us to see that the grace that has saved us is the meaning of the universe and therefore ought to be shared with everyone).

The closer we get to God through Jesus, the more the Spirit cultivates in us humility and love for God and neighbor. If we do not focus on the humbling, empowering gospel of grace and if, in fact, we stay "religious," we get puffed up in our own achievements and successes and lost in our own self-righteousness, and our hearts grow colder both to God and to our neighbors. Even if we are engaged in spiritual pursuits, if we are focused on ourselves, we end up only using God and using others. And if you're using people, you certainly aren't loving them. Only the gospel gives us the security (of union with Christ) to risk reputation and hurt in order to love others sacrificially and boldly.

2. Be Ye Joyful

We think joy is a feeling. In a way, it is. But in the Bible joy is both a command of the law and an implication of the gospel.

Over and over again, worshipers of God are commanded to rejoice. A sampling:

> And you shall take on the first day the fruit of splendid trees, branches of palm trees and boughs of leafy trees and willows of the brook, and you shall rejoice before the LORD your God seven days. (Lev. 23:40)

> And you shall sacrifice peace offerings and shall eat there, and you shall rejoice before the LORD your God. (Deut. 27:7)

> This is the day that the LORD has made;
>   let us rejoice and be glad in it. (Ps. 118:24)

> So if a person lives many years, let him rejoice in them all. (Eccles. 11:8)

> But be glad and rejoice forever
>   in that which I create. (Isa. 65:18)

> Shout, O Israel!
> Rejoice and exult with all your heart. (Zeph. 3:14)

> Rejoice greatly, O daughter of Zion! (Zech. 9:9)

> Rejoice in hope, be patient in tribulation, be constant in prayer. (Rom. 12:12)

> Rejoice with those who rejoice. (Rom. 12:15)

> Likewise you also should be glad and rejoice with me. (Phil. 2:18)

> Rejoice in the Lord always; again I will say, rejoice. (Phil. 4:4)

> Rejoice always. (1 Thess. 5:16)

But rejoice insofar as you share Christ's sufferings. (1 Pet. 4:13)

> Let us rejoice and exult
> and give him the glory,
> for the marriage of the Lamb has come,
> and his Bride has made herself ready. (Rev. 19:7)

Finally, brothers, rejoice. (2 Cor. 13:11)

And yet what God has commanded of us, he also gifts us as an entailment of salvation.

Through him we have also obtained access by faith into this grace in which we stand, and we rejoice in hope of the glory of God. (Rom. 5:2)

Rejoice that your names are written in heaven. (Luke 10:20)

Rejoice and be glad, for your reward is great in heaven. (Matt. 5:12)

> In your presence there is fullness of joy;
> at your right hand are pleasures forevermore. (Ps. 16:11)

God is not expecting us to muster up happiness in him from the void of some nebulous religious inclinations, from the black hole of our empty emotional reservoir. He puts the joy inside of us that he demands from us. What grace! "These things I have spoken to you," Jesus says, "that my joy may be in you, and that your joy may be full" (John 15:11).

I want a full joy. How about you?

When we come to see that Christ, through his gospel, satisfies the root of every desire, we get this joy, which we have been previously seeking everywhere but in Christ.

3. Be Ye Peaceful

The world is set against our peace. The world wants us desperately afraid. And we don't need any help with this. We are naturally, each in our own way, restless and fearful people.

When we first become Christians, we typically experience the newness of belief with all its attendant zeal and enthusiasm. We feel most keenly in the fresh wake of our conversion the boldness that ought to accompany one who has escaped death and has been eternally rescued. But then days go by and the walk begins to feel more routine, more mundane. The "normal Christian life" begins to make us feel more . . . well, normal. The things of earth grow strangely bright. We hear competing messages; the noise of the world, the noise of our accuser, the noise of our internal anxieties, and the noise of our insecurities begin to challenge the still, small voice of God. The things of God become less comfortable than the offerings of daily life in the world. The vision of God's promise of eternal life, which drove our faith so strongly in the beginning, starts to wane and perhaps seems less compelling, less immediately gratifying than the promises of the things around us. And as the fulfillment of the promise seems to delay day by day, so the opportunities for doubt and discouragement seem to grow.

The truth is there is *always* something to be afraid of. And the more bored you are with the things of God, the more vulnerable you will be to this fear when difficulty comes.

And this is why you can hardly go anywhere in the Bible without bumping into the words, "Don't be afraid." Some say it's the most frequent command in the Scriptures. Paul says that the Spirit grows peace inside of us. Over time, as we walk with Jesus, we begin to see more and more of the ways he is loving us and more and more of the ways he is working in the world, and the cross looms more largely over our sin and the empty tomb looms more largely over the mess and dysfunction of the world. And the impulse to rest in him becomes more immediate. The heart's "muscle memory" toward the gospel gets quicker and stronger.

As with joy, peace is not just commanded but actually given: "Peace I leave with you; my peace I give to you. Not as the world gives do I give to you. Let not your hearts be troubled, neither let them be afraid" (John 14:27).

If, indeed, he has overcome the world, we can "take heart." We can take the heart he himself has given us!

This peaceful heart results when we realize that, according to God himself, we are reconciled to him and no longer at enmity, because his Son's blood has pardoned us, purified us, and pacified us. Peace between us and God comes through propitiation, and if we are at peace with God and have peace from God, what in the world should we be afraid of?

4. Be Ye Patient

At its root, impatience is confusion about control. Impatience is the rotten fruit of self-sovereignty. We are impatient because people and circumstances do not tend to operate as if we are the center of the universe. In fact, if we believe we are the center of the universe, we will find that even people who treat us well end up testing our patience. There is no holiness so fickle as the false holiness of the self-righteous. So how does the gospel cultivate patience in us?

It begins with that same humbling we spoke of earlier. The gospel puts us in our place. We are sinners who stand only by the virtue of grace. We are saved by Christ alone. Knowing this helps us climb down from our pedestals. It's at the top that we mistakenly inflate our own sense of importance. Coming down to see that the ground is level at the foot of the cross helps us regard others with more thoughtfulness—and more patience.

The unilateral salvation of the gospel of grace also reminds us that our life belongs totally and ultimately to God. We are reminded, in the sovereignty of salvation by grace, of the sovereignty of the God of grace. He is the one upholding the universe (Heb. 1:3). He is the one in control. He created the world and called it good, and he will see it to its predetermined end and new beginning. And if this God who is ordaining all things can be trusted—if he is good and loving and also just and wise—who are we to be impatient with the way things are going? Who are we to be impatient with others? Do we reckon God incapable or incompetent to appoint the kings of the nations, to predetermine the course of our days and years, to make sure that all ends up the way he wants it all to end up?

If the God of our salvation is sovereign, we can relax. It doesn't depend on us. The world is not what we make of it. I can stop fuming about the lady in front of me in the grocery store express line with forty-six *more* items than the allotted ten. I might have freely chosen this line but God saw this moment coming. He predestined this very circumstance. If I believe that, I can be patient.

Over time, following Jesus cultivates a quicker retreat to patience in us. The Spirit produces more and more patience in our hearts, because as we grow in faith we also grow in our realization of our sin. We see more of our inadequacy as we mature in Jesus, not less. Our subsequent humility results in patience with God (who is astoundingly patient with our sinful selves) and with others as we become more inclined to let them off the hook.

5. Be Ye Kind

So this is the story of how J. I. Packer made me cry. Sort of. It starts like this: I once had the great privilege of contributing to a Bible study series by writing the entry for Paul's Letter to the Romans. I was intimidated by the prospect from the very beginning, but my editor assured me I was not contacted by mistake, that indeed they didn't want that other "Jared Wilson" or somebody smarter, but actually me. And even though I was further intimidated by the fact that the series editor was none other than the aforementioned evangelical giant Dr. Packer, I studied and wrote my little heart out and produced a slim little volume with which both the publisher and myself were happy. Then I went back to minding my own business.

Later I was visiting with my friend Matt, who had written another entry in the series, and we were reminiscing about our experiences when he mentioned that our editor had sent him Packer's notes on his manuscript. I was like, "Hold up. What? That's an actual thing that's possible?" I was instantly jealous. And curious. I thought to myself, *Why didn't they send me Packer's edits on* my *manuscript?*

The answers I entertained varied. Maybe he was hands-on with certain submissions but not all of them. Maybe my manuscript pages were lost. I assumed it was more than likely, however, that my manuscript was terrible and the pages had become bloody with Packer's savage editorial pen, and the publisher was just protecting me from getting my feelings hurt. But I had to know. So I wrote to the editor and said, very pitifully, "Hey, Matt got his manuscript with Packer's edits. Could I have mine?"

The next day a FedEx package arrived at my office. *Okay, then.*

I worked the pages from their plastic pouch with fear and trembling and started thumbing through them. Turns out I didn't have much to worry about. Packer's pen was light and friendly. Most of his corrections had to do with word choices or expansions of my thinking, adding the clarity and theological precision he has always been known for.

But then I came to it. Page 18. There, at the bottom of that page, as I was expounding on Romans 2:4, I had written this:

> In yet another wonderful affirmation of where the source of power to change is found, Paul reminds us in Romans 2:4 that "God's kindness is meant to lead you to repentance." Not his law, not his berating, not his exasperation or his cajoling. His kindness.[3]

Period. End of thought.

But Dr. Packer had added one thin, vertical pen stroke, turning my period into an exclamation point and underlining it to show the change. It's not God's kindness—yawn—that leads us to repentance, but God's *kindness*! Exclamation point!

I couldn't stop looking at the correction. And then I began to cry. And I'll tell you why. Twelve years ago, when I was at the bottom of the barrel and the bottom of my life and felt useless and worthless and unlovable and didn't want to even be alive anymore, I could not have imagined in my wildest dreams that someday I'd be staring at something I had written that had been edited by J. I. Packer. If you had said that to me then, I would have laughed at you and then punched you (probably). I had no capacity for such things. And as I stared at this edited sentence—just this one little pen stroke that makes a world of difference—in a cushioned chair behind my big desk at Midwestern Baptist Theological Seminary, I started crying, remembering what it was like to be face down on the floor of my guest bedroom wishing I was dead.

Because it was in that very experience that God put an exclamation point where I had put a period. Indeed, that entire terrible despair was the rotten fruit of my own sinful choices and my own inner darkness.

But God! His kindness! It led me to repentance.

I am grateful for these reminders, the big ones and the little ones, that help me not take the grace of God lightly. The gospel is an exclamation point.

The more we experience the kindness of God in and through our own repentance, the more kindness we find to afford others. To be unkind to others, in fact, is to disbelieve God's kindness and to spit on it. For a follower of Jesus to be unkind to others is to depict Jesus as unkind. But indeed, because the almighty God has provided us with his inexhaustible kindness, we find an ever-deepening well of kindness for others.

6. Be Ye Good

Oh no, now here's a tricky one. Because just as most every human in the world believes themselves to be loving enough, most every human in the world tends to believe they are *good* enough too. And, in fact, it's Bible verses calling us to be good that are taken out of context to distort the true and essential message of Christianity.

If you were to go up to a stranger right now and ask them what the message of the Christian religion is, I would bet good money they'd tell you some variation of the command "Be good."

We reinforce this misunderstanding often enough. When Christians complain about the sinfulness of unbelievers, when we parade our own good deeds in small and big ways, when we treat others as beneath us, we are communicating in very powerful ways that being good is the point of our faith.

What does it even mean to "be good"? How would one know if he or she is good?

I mean, how good is good enough? Can we consider ourselves good if we just do some good things? Can we adopt the Boy Scouts' ethic of one good deed per day? Or to be considered good do we need to do lots of good things? What constitutes "a lot"? If we do more good things than bad things? How would we even begin to measure this?

The mind boggles at the sheer uncertainty of it all. It's undoubtedly possible for every human being to do good things. But how could anyone know for sure that he or she is a good person?

Part of the good news is that being good is not the point of our faith. Being good is not even possible apart from faith.

The Reformers taught—rightly, I believe—that *justification* is the article of doctrine upon which the church will rise or fall. But how can anyone be justified?

How can anyone be justified when the Bible is clear that no one is good? Not a single one of us does good (Rom. 3:12). And yet we rail against the worldliness of the world as if the world could in its own power become good, and we load up our worship services with practical applications, giving short shrift to the gospel, as if "being good" were the point of Christianity.

I'll tell you what's good—the news that reminds us that being good isn't the point.

Jesus won't even let us call *him* good without dealing with the implications of it.

> And as he was setting out on his journey, a man ran up and knelt before him and asked him, "Good Teacher, what must I do to inherit eternal life?" And Jesus said to him, "Why do you call me good? No one is good except God alone." (Mark 10:17–18)

Now, Jesus isn't saying that he isn't good. But he's wanting this guy to connect the dots. He wants him, first of all, to stop throwing the word *good* around like it applies to anything and everything, as if it's something easily achieved by our gifts and talents or even our positions and platforms. By saying that only God is good, Jesus is saying that no normal human being is good. So if we (rightly) determine that Jesus is good, it should not simply be because he's an incredible teacher or, as the world tends to see him, an inspirational guru or enlightened life coach. If we call Jesus good it is only because we call him God.

And if we are to be good, if we are to have the goodness Paul says comes from the Holy Spirit (Gal. 5), it can only be because we've been connected to the very goodness of Jesus by the Spirit.

In ourselves none of us stands justified. In Christ we are justified. In the gospel his goodness becomes ours.

So along with the article of justification we must include the incredible doctrine of *imputation*. Justification speaks to our right standing *before* God. We've been forgiven; we've been declared righteous. But imputation speaks to our righteousness *in* God (2 Cor. 5:21). We've not just been forgiven and declared righteous; we are in Christ actually made righteous. It's not just that God wipes our sinful slate clean (justification); he also writes onto the slate of our heart the perfect righteousness of Christ (imputation). We are made good as the alien goodness of Jesus is credited to our account as if it were our own.

And so the good deeds that result in our life through the Spiritual process of progressive sanctification are not ginned up, as it were, from our religious sensibilities or from "the goodness of our heart" but from the goodness of Jesus gradually taking more dominion in us.

7. Be Ye Faithful

I hope you are beginning to get the point. All the things God commands of Christians he himself supplies in abundance. Every demand put upon us by God is a binding demand; we aren't to shirk our responsibilities or grow passive in our pursuit of holiness. But every demand put upon us by God is ultimately and Spiritually fulfilled in us by God himself as he is determined, for his own glory, to deliver us to himself as righteous. This is no less true of the very faith that God requires to be in relationship with him.

If the essence of Christianity is not justification by "being good," it could be rightly said to be this: justification comes by grace alone, received through faith alone, in Christ alone.

The God who saves is holy and therefore commands us to place our faith in him for this salvation. And the God who saves is gracious and therefore gifts us the faith we need in order to be saved.

"Without faith it is impossible to please God," Hebrews 11:6 says. And yet, according to Ephesians 2:8, even this faith is a gift from God. It's as if God is saying, "You need faith to please me. Here, have some faith."

What a gracious God we have!

In fact, he is so gracious that even though our faith is imperfect and weird and wonky, he shores it up still and ever-more with his perfect grace and the perfect righteousness of his Son. Our faith could even be as small as a mustard seed, but so long as it's genuine it will still afford us the totality of Christ's eternal riches.

The saying is trustworthy, for:

> If we have died with him, we will also live with him;
> if we endure, we will also reign with him;
> if we deny him, he also will deny us;
> if we are faithless, he remains faithful—

for he cannot deny himself. (2 Tim. 2:11–13)

8. Be Ye Gentle

In 1 Timothy 6:11 Paul says to pursue gentleness. In Galatians 5 he says that the Spirit produces gentleness in us as we "walk by the Spirit" (v. 16) and are "led by the Spirit" (v. 18).

I will be honest in saying that I have found myself becoming more gentle due to the Spirit's working in me than in my own pursuit of gentleness. But I do have an ambition for it.

I tend to think, in fact, that by God's grace gentleness is often the result of just getting older as a believer, something that develops more in us as we simply slow down and become more wise, more circumspect, and more thoughtful.

I think of Jesus's encounter with the woman caught in adultery (John 8:1–11). The crowd had gathered with stones in hand to execute her. Jesus stoops down to doodle on the ground.

What did he write? I have no idea. (On a side note, I know the earliest Johannine manuscripts do not include this text, but I think this passage is a great authenticator of the historical reliability of the Gospels, as clearly the eyewitness to this event could not see what Jesus is writing and was honest about it. He or she could have easily made something up or speculated based on thirdhand information.) In any event, as Jesus is writing in the dirt, the crowd slowly drops their rocks and walks away. But it's the older people who walk away first (v. 9). Why?

As with Jesus's doodles in the dirt, we can only speculate. But I wonder if it's because the zeal of judgment is found most strongly in the young. When I was young(er), I knew everything. It was fantastic. There wasn't a subject I couldn't expound on and ignorance was no hindrance.

As I get older, I see more of my own sin and thus become more humble. As I get older, I see more of my own flaws and thus become more patient. As I get older, I see more of my own weakness and slowness and inadequacy and thus become more gentle.

"Take my yoke upon you," Jesus says, "and learn from me, for I am gentle and lowly in heart, and you will find rest for your souls" (Matt. 11:29).

Gentleness is inextricably connected to restfulness. So long as we are restless, so long as we are bucking against Christ's sovereignty, tugging at and stifling under his kindly yoke, we will not be shaped by his gentleness. But the more we rest in our salvation, in the security of our position in him for all eternity, the more gentle we will become. He is gentle with us. And his gentleness is conferred to us, transferred to us as we find him gentle in the face of our own stubbornness and failure to get our act together.

The more into his grace we rest, the more from his grace we will become gentle.

9. Be Ye Self-Controlled

From my current vantage point, as I write this very section, I can see a McDonald's drive-through lane across the parking lot. The McDonald's drive-through lane is where self-control goes to die. Everything is cheap, quick, and sickeningly satisfactory. The gratification is immediate, the ramifications less so. What keeps us from reaching out for the promise of instant satisfaction? What dulls our animal appetites?

It sounds counterintuitive on the surface of it. Paul calls this control "self-control," and yet he is clearly saying in context that this is a fruit grown by the Spirit. The fruit of self-control is at root *Spirit*-control—or, if you prefer, Spirit-led or Spirit-governed.

I have heard that the definition of maturity is the ability to delay gratification. Children don't get this. They are the very manifestation of immaturity. They want what they want when they want it, which is now. The best toy they can imagine is the one that they see somebody else holding. And we all know grown-ups who don't seem to have grown up beyond the impulses of their appetites.

Like patience and gentleness, self-control is cultivated in us as we grow in both years and in Christ. As we grow in Christ over the years, we have more and more opportunities to find our faith tested and to see how well his goodness stacks up against the petty offerings of the world. As we grow older in Christ, we have more opportunities to discover how lacking in lasting satisfaction things like money and sex and notoriety and anything else under the sun actually are. We see more of Christ's joy strong and steady against the seemingly endless stream of worldly happiness.

I think of Solomon in his masterpiece Ecclesiastes, looking back at his youth from the vantage point of old age, lamenting all the time he wasted in things that didn't last—things that at the time, from the vantage point of youth, seemed to offer so much. The more we walk with Christ and the more we are led by the Spirit, the less satisfying we find the world and so the more restrained we become with it.

Self-control is a fruit of the Spirit because those who abide in Christ have transformed desires. They want the satisfaction of Christ more and the gratification of the world less.

There's No Law against It

There you have it. The Nine Irrefutable Laws of Followship. As we've seen, because the Spirit produces these, we may as well call them promises as well as laws. They are irrefutable because Paul sums up this list of qualities—love, joy, peace, patience, kindness, goodness, faithfulness, gentleness, and self-control—with this curious little statement: "against such things there is no law" (Gal. 5:23).

What on earth can he mean by that?

Well, if we consider again the context of this passage, a letter to the Galatian church in general, we know that Paul is confronting a series of false teachings we might categorize as "legalism." But Paul is careful not to say that the gospel annihilates the law or ignores the law.

This is something those of us in the so-called gospel-centered tribe ought to constantly keep in mind. To be gospel-centered rather than law-centered is not to be law-avoiding, law-denying, or law-negating. No, instead, to be gospel-centered is to be law-fulfilling. In fact, what the testimony of Galatians and the bulk of New Testament teaching on law and gospel help us see is that centering on the good news of grace puts the law in its proper perspective and helps us adhere to it according to its design.

The law can tell us what to do but it cannot help us do it. The law cannot empower its own implications. The gospel, on the other hand, announces to us both Christ's fulfillment of the law and, by consequence, Christians' worshipful freedom to obey the law without fear of being crushed by it.

"Against such things there is no law" is Paul's way of saying that the fruit of the Spirit is how we demonstrate the law's fulfillment and the gospel's freedom. The law of God stands against drunkenness and sexual immorality and jealousy. But it is no hindrance to kindness and goodness and self-control because these qualities are demonstrations of the life the law was meant to reveal. The law does not stand against these things. It will not work against these things. (The law stands against sin, not life.) "I will put my law within them, and I will write it on their hearts," God says (Jer. 31:33).

And in the end, because God is determined to make us the holy people he commands us to be, we can be assured that not a single one of us who falls short of God's holy law in the flesh will be utterly lost in the Spirit.

The good news is that it is God who keeps us from failing; God ensures that we will stand before him blameless (Jude 24).

This means that, no matter how you feel, if you are a follower of Jesus you are never truly stuck. The Spirit is doing a million things in your heart and with your life, and while the theme song of your spiritual life may seem more like "Another One Bites the Dust" than "We Are the Champions," you are indeed growing. As Richard Sibbes says, "In the small seeds of plants lie hid both bulk and branches, bud and fruit."[4]

Jesus himself had some things to say about small seeds.

Your faith may be small and your walk may lack mileage, but he is with you every step of the way—and every stumble. And if you feel stuck, know he's right there beside you. He isn't one to ignore a child who's fallen into a hole (Luke 14:5).

Really, we can look at these nine qualities called the fruit of the Spirit and see a composite portrait of the perfectly fruitful man, the God-man Jesus Christ. He alone is the perfection of these things. He alone is the flawless manifestation of these virtues.

So we see that the Spirit is committed to making us more like Jesus. And in doing so, the Spirit is committed to making us more like the people we were designed to be.

The Holy Spirit is making us more like Jesus and at the same time more like our true selves.

8 Will the Real Me Please Stand Up?

(When You're Not Happy with the Person in the Mirror)

Now, by the help of God,
I shall become myself.

Søren Kierkegaard[1]

My gospel is a Narnian wardrobe. It seems simple enough from the outside—discernible, shaped, and dimensioned. But when I get myself inside of it, the dimensions expand. Its inside is bigger than its outside.

When Peter and Susan and Edmund and Lucy stepped into that wardrobe in their world and found themselves under the lamppost in Narnia, it wasn't just the new world that got bigger. They did too. They discovered an alternate space-time universe in which they weren't their ordinary schoolboy and schoolgirl selves. They discovered, in fact, that they were kings and queens. Going through the wardrobe grew them up in some peculiar way, matured them into truer versions of themselves. My gospel is like that.

My gospel is a time machine. Not like Kip Dynamite's time machine, ordered from some shady webpage, made of metal and wires, and prone to frying your gonads. No, the gospel is the real deal. It goes all the way back. And it goes all the way forward. At the same time, for all time. My gospel fits in my pocket, and yet when I grasp it with my trembling fist, it takes me everywhere and every*when*. It gets my name in the Lamb's book before time began and it puts my name over the door of some heavenly abode as yet unseen.

I'm getting ahead of myself.

I am grateful for the words that make up the gospel announcement, grateful for what they say about God, about life, about *me*. That tract in my childhood pocket was not a religious toaster manual. It was not a spiritual *Bazooka Joe* comic. It was simple and it was practical but it spanned all space and time. I don't have it anymore, but it still speaks a better word—an eternal word.

I'm a sufferer of words. When James calls the tongue a fire, I know what in the hell—phrasing intentional—he's talking about. I think many, many of us do. The fire may go out but its ashes smolder, sometimes for years and years, the smoke of its torment promising "forever."

When I was in high school, already well-neurotic from my own pronounced innate insecurities and well-battered by careless words from childhood onward, I remember being informed about a survey held by girls in the youth group at a sleepover. Apparently they were assembling in their imaginations "the perfect boy" using the composite parts of the boys in the youth group. I don't remember all whose parts were highlighted, but this adolescent Frankenhottie supposedly had my friend Kyle's chest and my friend Nicky's legs. (Who knew girls cared about *legs*?) It had other boys' eyes and arms and lips and hair—I recall hair being important—and who knows what else. The person telling me about this exercise then informed me that this imaginary object of desire had my personality.

I know this was meant to be seen as a compliment. But honestly. You know what "he/she has a good personality" is code for. What this news said to this skinny, insecure, pimply faced kid was this: *There is not a single physical part of you that is attractive. You are entirely ugly.*

Words sting. And bruise. I have trouble to this day remembering encouragement given to me, even though I know I receive it regularly. I even started an email folder called "Pick-Me-Ups" I can store kind words in, a place to revisit when I'm being stupid and forgetful to show myself, *See? People say nice things too.*

It's not them; it's me.

But I don't think this problem is all that rare. You likely suffer from it too. I can list quite easily the words that still haunt me:

"Stuttering wimp."—A female classmate on the playground, fifth grade

"Meet me after school, *bolio*."—A bully at the school I attended in the sixth grade, where white students were a distinct minority. (*Bolio* is Spanish for a kind of white bread, used as slang for basically "white boy.")

"You know that people can minister through writing too, right?"—A ministerial superior who treated me with passive aggression at some points and caustic third-degree interrogation at others, at this point unsubtly suggesting I wasn't cut out for "real" ministry.

"You weren't the first choice."—Person in the green room at a speaking engagement ten minutes before I was set to kick off the event.

"Misogynist; advocate of rape culture."—An especially painful (and especially *false*, I feel compelled to add) accusation hurled at me over the ramparts of the internet.

There are more. Some are too painful to share in print. Some are too profane. Some are water under the bridge and forgiveness in these instances means not reminding people who may be reading this of the pain caused. Some are just none of your business. But there are lots more, lots worse. And I'm sure you have them too.

Some of the painful things said to us are malicious and some are not. Some are true things, some half true, some not-at-all true. But they all hurt in their own ways, don't they? And the devil does one thing with these words: he turns them into fear and shame. The devil can turn even constructive criticism into a false accusation.

I know the words of the gospel. The problem is that too often the words of the accuser(s) are on video, as I've heard Tim Keller say, while the words of the gospel are on audio.

Identity Crisis

I used to love coming home from school and watching reruns of the TV show *Gilligan's Island*. I know you remember it. Seven castaways on a deserted island in the South Pacific, having been lost at sea after a storm: Gilligan, the skipper (too), the millionaire and his wife, the movie star, the professor, and Mary Ann. The episodes of *Gilligan's Island* got progressively weirder. I mean, not "find a hatch and punch in the numbers" weird, but more like goofy weird. In the beginning the castaways spent most of their time trying to get off the island. Thanks to the professor they were able to make rafts out of leaves, radios out of coconuts, even cars out of bamboo. But they couldn't get off the island. Eventually the writers had to come up with shenanigans on the island itself.

In the later seasons, the castaways discover a haunted house on the other side of the island. How they never discovered it before, I don't know, but I remember a mad scientist trying to swap their brains or something. One time the Harlem Globetrotters ended up on the island. Like I said: *goofy*. But the weirdest episode I remember—at least, I thought it was really weird—was one that begins with the gang noticing that things are going missing, which leads to Gilligan getting attacked, which leads to them discovering that there's a Japanese soldier hiding out on the island who still thinks it's World War II.

I thought that was completely ludicrous. Until I discovered it was based in reality!

There were several soldiers, actually, that we know of—the last remaining were Hiroo Onoda and Teruo Nakamura. Even though the Japanese surrendered to the Allies in 1945, these men refused, holding out like hermits in uniform for decades. Onoda camped out in the jungles of the Philippines until 1974(!), when his former commander finally came to inform him he could stop fighting. Nakamura fought his own private war in Indonesia until he was arrested in late 1974.

These guys spent thirty years fighting a war that was over. It's funny but it's not. *I* spent thirty years fighting a war that was over, struggling to believe God could love me, struggling to believe God could even stomach me, warring with the devil over where I belonged, warring with myself over where I stood. So many of the sinful patterns that plagued my life for so long arose from the mistaken belief that my soul was in some kind of spiritual limbo.

I was facing a crisis of identity. A question of reality. Who am I? *Whose* am I?

I believe that doing flows from being. Behavior problems are belief problems. Who or what you believe yourself to be will direct how you live. So when I finally, after thirty years as a Christian, discovered the doctrine of union with Christ, I felt like an unfrozen caveman discovering fire.

> If then you have been raised with Christ, seek the things that are above, where Christ is, seated at the right hand of God. . . . For you have died, and your life is hidden with Christ in God. (Col. 3:1, 3)

If you're a Christian, you're *here.* I know, because you're reading this book. You're in your office or on your couch or on an airplane or in a coffee shop or on the toilet. You're here. But if you're a Christian, you're also—in a very real sense—*there.*

Your true self is hidden with Christ in God.

Part of resting in the reality that your true self is hidden with Christ in God is looking at the true self you keep hiding inside yourself.

I recently resigned from pastoral ministry. Lord willing, I will take it up again someday, but for the moment I am on an indefinite sabbatical from vocational ministry. I took my first ministry position over twenty years ago, the summer I graduated high school, serving as youth minister for Zion Chinese Baptist Church in Houston, Texas. I have been in and out of ministry positions over the years, but after leaving our little church plant in Nashville, Tennessee, in 2009 to move to Vermont, I believed we had finally come home. I was not looking beyond that place. In my heart and mind, I had come to live and die with Middletown Springs Church. I joked about them having to pry the pulpit from my cold, dead hands. I believed it! I thought I'd finally arrived. I thought I was *there*.

But the joke was on me.

Easter 2015 was the first Easter in nine years I hadn't preached a resurrection sermon. That didn't dawn on me until Passion week. I had mixed feelings about it. A big part of me missed it, of course. But a big part of me also understands Christ's resurrection doesn't need me. I honestly do not want to be the kind of preacher who is like the rooster that thinks the sun is rising because he's crowing. I didn't have a sermon to prepare, didn't have several excellent points to proclaim—and what do you know? The sun came up Easter Sunday anyway. Christ was risen, indeed.

On my last Sunday in the Middletown Church pulpit, February 15, 2015, I preached on Genesis 22. Why? Because I had begun preaching through Genesis more than a year prior and I saw no reason why my leaving should disrupt the plan. I didn't know when I began that journey that Genesis 22 would be the end of the line for me, but the Lord did. And he has a wonderful sense of humor.

The narrative we find in Genesis 22, of Abraham taking his son Isaac up the mountain to sacrifice him at the Lord's command, is the earliest Bible story I remember wrestling with. I couldn't have been more than seven years old, and I distinctly recall looking at the classic illustration in my Bible storybook of Abraham with his knife poised over Isaac, who was bound to a stone altar. And I remember thinking, in a childlike way, *This is hard.* Even then I realized it would be an impossible thing if God asked me to kill someone I loved.

What I didn't realize then but do now is that *the hardness is the point.* This story is as hard as the atonement. Most of us can see the direct correlation to our heavenly Father offering up his only begotten Son to death.

So I finished up my tenure at Middletown Church preaching the earliest text I remember battling mentally with. I confess that after thirty-some years I have not found it any more comfortable. But in an odd way I found it comforting.

I found it comforting, even though preaching Genesis 22 on February 15 was my own journey up the mountain, knife in hand.

I have already mentioned how Dietrich Bonhoeffer's thoughts about the "wish dream" strike me as crucially helpful. Again, the wish dream is basically what the Bible calls *idolatry.* And the thing about idolatry, the thing about wish dreams, is that we so identify with them we lose all true bearings about ourselves. Often, we don't know who we are apart from them.

We all have wish dreams about just about everything in our life—we have wish-dream jobs, wish-dream spouses, wish-dream families, wish-dream lives. And we're constantly comparing the wish-dream versions of these things with the versions we actually have. Many a marriage struggles because spouses keep holding each other up against the impossible standard of the wish dream. And many a pastor struggles because he keeps holding the church he's been stewarded against his wish dream of the church he wants.

If you find yourself constantly measuring, constantly frustrated, constantly seeing all you don't have, Bonhoeffer actually says this is a good predicament, because it puts you on the verge of having your wish dream shattered and finally facing reality. The identity crisis can be a good thing.

All of Abraham's hopes and dreams were bound up in Isaac. Isaac was the child God promised. Isaac was the child Abraham and Sarah had schemed to conceive in ways other than by God's providence. Isaac was his parents' wish dream. And I imagine Abraham had a vision for how God's promise to multiply his descendants and expand his legacy into eternity would play out, and I imagine this lonely scenario of taking the wish dream up the mountain to slay it was not it.

We all have a vision for how life is supposed to go, what life is supposed to be like—what we want and how we want it and the way we want to feel about it—but then actual life happens, and when our heart is tuned to only find joy in the dream we will never find joy, because we've placed it in a mirage.

My vision for my ministry career was a mirage. I had a dream about the way I would wind up my ministry in Vermont, and it wasn't to spend six years there before moving to the Midwest!

It can be okay when pieces of our wish dreams come true, and some of us might actually get the whole shebang, but it's also dangerous to dwell in that imaginary world, because when our joy is placed anywhere but in Christ, we are setting ourselves up for incredible, crushing disappointment and spiritual and emotional disaster. When I believed God was asking me to quit my job, I felt this internal crisis in an unbelievably strong way. He might as well have commanded me to put a knife in it.

God asked me to quit. And when he did, he killed my dream.

I knew full well that ministry can become an idol. But if you had asked me about it at any point before I was contemplating God's call to leave the ministry, I would have assured you that, of all my idols, ministry was not on the list!

Isaac was, in one way, an idol for Abraham. Abraham's whole life had revolved so much around the hope of Isaac. He kept whining to God about it. So, looking at Genesis 22 leading up to my last Sunday, the Sunday I officially quit, I dared to ask myself, *How would I know what my real idols are?*

Well, one of the litmus test questions I've been fond of giving out to others in diagnosing idolatry is this: What, if taken away from you, would cause you a great crisis of identity?

I didn't know how much pastoral ministry was an idol for me until I believed God was asking me to set it aside. I could talk a great game about idolatry and I could talk a great game about pastors finding their justification in Christ alone, but then God had the audacity to actually test me on this! He actually asked me to set it aside.

I wanted to know, "For how long, God? For what time?" He wouldn't say; he still hasn't said. So I don't know.

And then my worry kicked in. Because that's one of the questions I worried about being asked: How long are you going to be out of pastoral ministry? And don't you know, in the months since my announcement, numerous people have asked me this, with varying levels of concern? I have been flattered and encouraged by their sense of "missing" my ministry but also greatly cautioned by what I self-righteously perceived in it, as well—namely this: *If I'm not in pastoral ministry, what am I?*

I started thinking of all the things people would say. I started to suffer from imaginary words.

"I thought you were the New England guy."

"I thought you were the small church guy."

"I thought you were the rural church guy."

"I thought you said not to confuse difficulty with lack of calling. Isn't that what you're doing?"

"I thought you were the 'pastor's justification' guy. And now you're quitting?"

Like Abraham's wife, Sarah, I worried about the laughter of others. I worried about their criticism, their questions, their disapproval. That's a big one for me: disapproval.

But ten years ago God broke into that little guest bedroom where suicidal me was crying and praying my guts out, and he grabbed hold of me and proclaimed by his Spirit, *I love you and I approve of you.*

I lost my taste for lots of things in that moment, and one of those was trying to "get better" by the law. We ask for bread and God doesn't give us stones. I learned there, in the rubble of my dreams for my life, my ministry, my everything—the rubble of myself—that Christ is all and that trying to measure up is garbage.

This is why, for all my screwups as a pastor, all my sins and weaknesses, I can still boast in Christ. I can say that no one can say I didn't faithfully beat the drum of Christ's finished work. Because I know it is our only hope. The gospel of Jesus Christ is our only hope and security of enduring approval, of eternal validation, of spiritual fulfillment, of eternal joy.

So as hard as it has been to take my Isaac up the mountain and lay the wood on his back and tie him to the altar and raise the knife, I can do so, because I know God will provide—and I know God has provided.

So when my wife and I heard him say, *Set this aside. Give this to me*, I was thinking of all that people would say, all the dreams I had for dying in Vermont or raising up a successor and passing the baton, and how I didn't want to see those dreams die, but in the end we gathered up our meager faith and said, "Here we are, Lord. Whatever you want."

My availability to God's call to sacrifice—Abraham's availability to God's call to sacrifice, *your* availability to God's call to sacrifice—is predicated on understanding that God doesn't need any more messiahs. He sent one. The job is finished. We are not needed. I am not needed.

Ah, but I'm *wanted*.

That's liberating, isn't it? To not be needed but wanted?

What wish dream do you need to put a knife in?

Do you imagine that your life would feel more fulfilling if you had a different job? A better spouse? Do you think you'll finally feel like you've "arrived" when you have a certain amount of money in the bank or a certain title on your office door? Are you constantly comparing your life to the pictures you see on Instagram and Facebook?

Maybe it's time to take those visions—these idols—up the mountain.

What false version of yourself do you need to crucify?

Do you see the love God has for you in the sacrifice he did not spare? The Lord took his only Son, his Son whom he loves, up the mountain and there was no ram in the thicket. Jesus even cried out for one, praying, "If there's any other way, Father!"

But he was the way.

Jesus Loves the Real You

I think of Jesus with the rich ruler (Luke 18:18–30). This guy wanted Jesus to accept everything he was *willing* to give. But Jesus knew what was in his heart, and so he asked for that.

This is how you know what your god really is; this is how you know what's really the treasure of your heart. What is it that you wouldn't give up for Jesus? You'd give up everything in the world but this one thing.

Well, that's what you worship.

The real you is an idolater. And the claims of Jesus upon your life will reveal to you where your true affections lie.

Do you know what else will do this? Suffering.

When hardship comes, when sickness comes, when trouble comes, our true selves are revealed. What we really worship is revealed. Stress does this too. Irritations. Inconveniences. People and circumstances frustrating our wish dreams, interrupting our self-established agendas, challenging our self-styled sovereignty.

Every time we lose our temper, we show our true self. "Oh, that wasn't me!" we plead. "I'm so sorry, I lost my temper. I wasn't myself."

Yes you were! That was the real you, finally. That was the realest you've been! Losing your temper is losing the pretense that you're actually a good person.

The real you is the you who comes out in times of trouble. As Charles Spurgeon said, "Trials teach us what we are; they dig up the soil, and let us see what we are made of."[2]

The biblical image for this is a clay jar. Paul says we carry our treasures inside ourselves as if in "jars of clay" (2 Cor. 4:7). Why? Because we are fragile, and when we are broken what's inside is revealed. What we worship shows through.

Every time we take a hit, our true self comes out. We can try to hide it in times of comfort and ease, but we can't keep our true self covered. The jar will crack. The fig leaves will rot and fall. Your true, rotten self will come out.

But here's the good news. That real you, the you inside that you hide, the you that you try to protect, the you that you hope nobody sees or knows—*that's* the you that God loves.

No, he doesn't love your sin, of course. But he loves your true self. Without pretense, without façade, without image management, without the religious makeup. You the sinner, you the idolater, you the worshiper of false gods—*that's the you Jesus loves.*

Look, this is the whole point of the Christian message: God loves sinners.

Jesus died for sinners. He didn't wait for us to get our act together. (He knew we never could!)

> While we were still weak, at the right time Christ died for the ungodly . . . while we were still sinners, Christ died for us. (Rom. 5:6, 8)

Every other religion in the world has man in the gutter trying to figure out how to get to heaven; only Christianity has heaven coming down to the gutter.

Real talk, coming at you now: *you are more sinful than you realize but you are also more loved than you know.*

This is what Martin Luther meant when he said to "sin boldly." You ever hear that he said that? It's confusing. Is Luther saying to go on sinning, which Paul says not to do in Romans 6:1–2? I don't think so. I think Luther meant that because the good news is true, we can boldly admit that we are sinners!

So long as we are looking down at ourselves, we go into self-protection mode. But when we look up we can own up!

Once we discover that grace is oxygen, we can breathe freely. The reality of our true, sinful self doesn't have to define us. We don't have to hide it but we don't have to be ruled by it either!

In Martin Luther's *Letters of Spiritual Counsel*, we find these words of encouragement written to a young correspondent:

> When the devil throws our sins up to us and declares that we deserve death and hell, we ought to speak thus: "I admit that I deserve death and hell. What of it? Does this mean that I shall be sentenced to eternal damnation? By no means. For I know One who suffered and made satisfaction in my behalf. His name is Jesus Christ, the Son of God. Where he is, there shall I be also."[3]

And there is the key to following Jesus not as a defeated person but as a person of confidence, of hope, of glory: you are free to own up to your true sinful self because you are *set free* from your true sinful self.

Becoming Who You Are

Yes, I say: the gospel is a time machine. It unites us to the omnipresent Christ forever. Not that we become omnipresent like him and not that we become somehow "like God." That's a damnable aspiration. But we are somehow, by the ministry of the Spirit and by virtue of our union with Christ, fashioned more and more into his likeness (2 Cor. 3:18). We don't become of the essence of God but we do somehow "become partakers of the divine nature" (2 Pet. 1:3–4).

I see this time-defying gospel in 1 Corinthians 15, where Paul says in verse 1 that we received the gospel (past) and stand in the gospel (present), but also in verse 2 that we *are being saved* by the gospel (present-future). In a very real way—because to say something is a Spiritual reality is not to say that it is less real but actually more real—we are already sanctified (1 Cor. 6:11) despite the fact that we also are *being* sanctified.

Sinners who trust in Jesus, since we are presently united to the risen, ascended, enthroned Jesus Christ, are recipients of and sharers in his perfect righteousness. So God never has to look for your holiness. You may see yourself as worthless and faithless, but God never has to look for your righteousness, because since you have been raised with Christ and since Christ is seated at God's right hand, your holiness is also seated at his right hand.

And if you are hidden with Christ in God, then you have nothing left to hide. You are free to be you. The real you.

This is eschatological stuff. This is end-times stuff!

The eschatological tension of "already" and "not yet" is as true of you as it is of the world. Only you will not be left behind. In fact, you can't be, because in a real way, you are already there.

You. Are. Already. There.

Let me say it again: you're here. But you're also *there*. Really, you're just waiting for yourself to show up. When it's all said and done, in some way you're going to get there and you'll already be there waiting to greet yourself, and yourself is going to say to yourself, "I'm so glad you're here! You made it! Now we can finally be a whole person."

Oh, I can't wait to be a whole person!

To be a whole person. Don't you long for that?

And the good news of union with Christ means it will happen. It *is* happening.

"When I come to God," Mike Hawkins says, "he makes me more of a person. He makes me who I am."[4]

And here lies the sweet, complicated irony of the Christian life: over time we each become more and more like Jesus while at the same time becoming more and more our true selves.

And now we're beginning to see how deep this gospel really is. Because it doesn't just give us forgiveness of sins. And it doesn't just give us the righteousness of Christ. And it doesn't just unite us eternally to Christ. And it doesn't just promise us the work of spiritual sanctification throughout our life. It also promises us the hope of glory when all is said and done.

Winding Down, Looking Up

I remember the exact moment I got old. I recently entered my forties, which means I'm in that weird age limbo where old folks still consider me young but genuinely young people have started calling me "sir" and otherwise ignoring me, which means I'm actually *not* young. Every morning something new hurts. I guess they call this middle age. I am getting less young. But the precise moment in time I suddenly turned old was actually several years ago.

My first mistake was agreeing to play full-court basketball. I had played full-court basketball plenty of times before. I figured it'd be no sweat (figuratively speaking). I used to ball with the best of the couch potatoes. I had, as they say, "game" (relatively speaking).

The first sign something was wrong was just how quickly I got winded. Something had happened to my endurance, my stamina. But I was hanging in there. Then, at one point in the game, while we were on defense, a teammate of mine stole the ball and began heading up court. I cut a quick line up and to his right, across the court. He saw me breaking and threw a beautiful football pass over a couple of reversing defenders, and I stretched my arms out to catch in stride.

So far, so good.

As I caught the ball and began to dribble, eyes toward the paint, a defender crossed my path. As he began to match my offensive pace with his defensive backpedal, my brain said, *Fake left, go right.*

It's something I'd done plenty of times before. You don't even have to think about it when you're young and fit. It's like riding a bike, playing a video game, whatever. It's muscle memory. You aren't pondering it or strategizing it. Your brain sends the impulse to do it, and you do it. Quickly, smoothly, successfully.

So my brain said, *Fake left, go right.*

My body said, *Yeah, we're not going to do that.*

Well, my body actually, definitively said, *We're not going to do that right now, and we're not going to do that, like, ever again.*

And I actually fell down. Straight down, flat on my face. My legs felt like rubber and I collapsed onto the court.

The ball rolled away pathetically.

One of my teammates came over to help me up and said, "What happened?"

I looked at him and said, "I don't know. I think I just got old."

I don't know about you, but I am very much looking forward to that resurrection body.

One day, when the Lord returns and vanquishes sin, sickness, grief, injustice, and death itself, we who are united to Christ will receive a body like his. Like ours, but like his. Tangible, real, fleshy. And yet perfect, spiritual, glorious.

Oh, man, am I looking forward to this resurrection body!

But I'll tell you what: I'm looking forward more to having this stench of failure and this dark cloud of disapproval *gone.*

With one puff of breath from the mouth of Jesus—*pfftt!*—gone. And I'm free.

"If then you have been raised with Christ, seek the things that are above, where Christ is, seated at the right hand of God" (Col. 3:1).

To find pleasure, satisfaction, meaning, or purpose in anything and everything under the sun is like chasing wind or trying to catch smoke. It's like worshiping flakes of rust or bowing down at a powdery mound of dust. In and through the gospel we know that all of the things we actually long for can only be found in God.

His Son, Jesus, is the apex and sum of all that is good and lovely and wonderful. To get lost in him is to finally find one's true self. You can't find yourself anywhere else or in anyone else.

But here we are. Struggling along. Enjoying more of the dead and putrid things than we ought. Fighting sin—or, more often than not, surrendering to it. Our true sinful self keeps poking through the cracks. Every time trouble comes and every time irritations and frustrations come, our real self rises up.

And we—you and I—are terrible repenters. We don't even know all the stuff we ought to repent of. None of us will get to that heavenly finish line perfectly repented.

So we will finish our days basically crawling across that finish line, dragging our sorry self into heaven, and the Lord who is our righteousness will be standing there, looking down over us, mighty hands on his hips, and he will say, "Well done."

I don't know what you do with this, but I can't yawn at it. It makes me stagger. That the holy God of the universe, to whom I owe my very life, would punish his own Son so he wouldn't have to punish me is *staggering*. Because he loves me.

And that Jesus, the only Son of God, would go up that mountain called Golgotha, not confused about where the sacrifice would come from but knowing *he* was the sacrifice—and go willingly—overcomes me by this truest of loves.

Yes, as Keller says, too often the words of the accuser(s) are on video and the gospel is on audio.

And so, like my friend Ray says to do, I stare at the glory of God until I see it. I am weak. If I hear anything long enough I will start to believe it. This works for gospel words too. So I stop listening to myself and start talking to myself, *preaching* to myself. I am not who they say I am; I am who God says I am, and I don't have to be an Osteen fanboy to say that and think that. I just have to be a Christian.

Let them come with their words, then. Let the devil come with his barrage of lies, even his truths-turned-lies. I rebuke him. I confound him. I may be in the ditch of Romans 7 but I throw Romans 8 at his sniveling little face. I've got a pretty good arm for such things, past high-school girls' judgment notwithstanding.

Satan comes with his wounding, haunting words, and I stand behind my advocate Christ the Lord. He gives me more words, better words, words more permanent than life:

I will give you rest (Matt. 11:28).

You are the apple of my eye (Zech. 2:8).

I take pleasure in you (Ps. 147:11).

You are more than a conqueror through me (Rom. 8:37).

I am not ashamed to call you my brother (Heb. 2:11).

I rejoice over you (Zeph. 3:17).

Hell will not prevail against you (Matt. 16:18).

The words like this don't stop. They go on and on. The Bible is full to brimming with good news for me, and the Spirit hammers the words into my heart. The words of fear and shame may cut deep, but Christ's blood speaks a better word (Heb. 12:24).

Be careful, little ears, what you hear.

How about some more Luther?

> The Prince of Darkness grim, we tremble not for
>   him;
> His rage we can endure, for lo, his doom is sure,
> One little word shall fell him.[5]

9

Does Grace Go All the Way Down?

(When You Wonder If It Could Get Any Worse)

It is better to go to the house of mourning
than to go to the house of feasting,
for this is the end of all mankind,
and the living will lay it to heart.

Ecclesiastes 7:2

My gospel sometimes feels as light as a feather. And when I feel frail and floating, it doesn't appear to hold much strength for me. When I am in the cold darkness, desperate for a hand to hold—for the arms of an embrace—the words of the gospel sometimes ring hollow, thin, tinny to my ears, as if echoing down the length of a long tunnel.

Will I ever get out? Will I ever see the light?

I long for an anchor in the storm. I long for a pillow on which to lay my head.

Everything is trying to bring you down. Do you ever feel this way? Everything is pressing you in, ratcheting up the tension, and just when you think you'll get a break, something else falls apart. And then *you* fall apart.

Back when I was going through the darkness of a depression so heavy I thought daily about killing myself, I could see no light at the end of the tunnel. I didn't even think I was in a tunnel. It felt more like a deep well—a pit, really. And down there at the bottom, I prayed in ways I'd never prayed before. I had reached the end of myself and had become desperate for God. I wanted to know if his grace was just for the well-adjusted people up on the surface. I wanted to know if his grace might actually go all the way down to me.

I think of that silly little story about the old woman challenging Bertrand Russell's presentation on the cosmos. This lady stood up after his talk and publicly repudiated the idea that the earth was a sphere revolving around the sun. No, she said, the earth was actually flat and rested on the back of a giant turtle. (Sometimes we have to reinvent reality when it feels so jarring to our own expectations.) Russell apparently quipped, "What is the turtle resting on?" to which the old woman quickly replied, "Young man, it's turtles all the way down."

Seems legit.

It makes me think of grace. (No, really.) Because when it comes to our dependence on God, it is all grace or no grace. If our standing with him rests even an ounce on our works, we are utterly and hopelessly lost. No, it must be grace all the way down.

We bring nothing to this relationship except our nothingness. We bring our emptiness and Christ brings his riches. We bring our pit and he brings his rope.

But sometimes we are tempted to think he'd just as soon hang us with it as help us.

I think of the apostle Paul. This man knew suffering. Like, he really, really suffered. In 2 Corinthians 11, he goes on a tear about the qualification of his hardships that blows our stupid complaints out of the water. He'd been sick, tortured, near death, and shipwrecked. He knew what it was like to be hated, starved, and attacked. Paul knew suffering.

And yet he was totally abandoned to Jesus. Something extraordinary had happened to him. One day, while he was minding his own religious business, he got hijacked by grace, waylaid by Jesus Christ. Paul stepped into the bear trap of the gospel. And, ever after, he was "all in." If he was in a pit, he was all in that pit. If that's what Jesus had for him, he was down for it. Because he didn't care if he lived or died, so long as he had Jesus.

It wasn't all suffering for Paul, but it was pretty close to all suffering. After his miraculous conversion he did seem to have a few other miraculous, ecstatic experiences—yet it is his pain and weakness he seems most keen to highlight. Consider this famous passage from his second letter to the Corinthian church, where he compares his present pain with a past pleasure:

> I must go on boasting. Though there is nothing to be gained by it, I will go on to visions and revelations of the Lord. I know a man in Christ who fourteen years ago was caught up to the third heaven—whether in the body or out of the body I do not know, God knows. And I know that this man was caught up into paradise—whether in the body or out of the body I do not know, God knows—and he heard things that cannot be told, which man may not utter. On behalf

of this man I will boast, but on my own behalf I will not boast, except of my weaknesses—though if I should wish to boast, I would not be a fool, for I would be speaking the truth; but I refrain from it, so that no one may think more of me than he sees in me or hears from me. So to keep me from becoming conceited because of the surpassing great-ness of the revelations, a thorn was given me in the flesh, a messenger of Satan to harass me, to keep me from becoming conceited. Three times I pleaded with the Lord about this, that it should leave me. But he said to me, "My grace is suf-ficient for you, for my power is made perfect in weakness." Therefore I will boast all the more gladly of my weaknesses, so that the power of Christ may rest upon me. For the sake of Christ, then, I am content with weaknesses, insults, hard-ships, persecutions, and calamities. For when I am weak, then I am strong. (2 Cor. 12:1–10)

Most of our life is spent in verses 7–9. I'm willing to bet none of our life is spent in verses 1–4. And as much as we'd like more information on this heavenly visitation (and we're going to come back to that bizarre little episode in our next, and final, chapter), Paul seems more interested in feeling his pain and expounding on his weakness. Because what Paul had experienced—and what he wants us to experience—is just how all-encompassing God's grace really is. He wants us to believe in the all-sufficiency of grace. He wants us to know that it's grace *all the way down.*

"What is grace resting on?" the scientist asks.

"Young man, grace is resting on grace."

Paul had experienced the discombobulating effect of the gospel's takeover of his life and in the whirlwind of God's glorious mission he had tasted a bit of heaven and his union with Christ there, and so as he's barreling into

2 Corinthians 12, he is building on the breathlessness punctuating the entire letter. In chapter 5 he references being out of his mind. In chapter 11 he starts in with the foolishness talk—"bear with me in a little foolishness" (v. 1) and so forth. Even in the pit of despair, he is swallowed up by grace. It is this sense of security despite his imminent death that in fact prompts him to boast not in his strength but in his weakness.

For Paul, less of himself is a good thing, because it means more of Jesus. For Paul, less of himself is not just tolerable but *preferable* if it means more of Jesus.

Despite all that's going on in 2 Corinthians 12:1–10—the mysteries of the vision and the thorn—the key verse, the key takeaway as far as I can see, is in verse 9: "But he said to me, 'My grace is sufficient for you, for my power is made perfect in weakness.'"

Now, *sufficiency* for Paul does not mean "good enough." When you and I say something is "sufficient," that's usually what we mean. We mean, "That'll be okay." Like when you're driving down the highway and you see a truck with a mattress tied perilously to the roof with a little bit of twine. Whoever tied that mattress down thought, *Yeah, that's sufficient.* But Paul doesn't say grace is sufficient in that way. When Paul says grace is sufficient, he means that grace is *all* we need. It's not "fine." It's more than enough.

> When thro' fiery Trials thy Pathway shall lie,
> My grace all sufficient shall be thy supply.[1]

It is grace that goes all the way down through our self-sufficiency and our self-righteousness, exposing them as rusty, feeble scaffolding indeed. It goes all the way down to meet us at our realest self, at our most vulnerable self, in the reservoir of our soul, in the deepest, darkest valleys of our heart—in our weakness and in our suffering.

Grace Goes All the Way Down to Our Deepest Need

Grace is all-sufficient for weakness.

"I must go on boasting," Paul says in verse 1. "On my own behalf I will not boast, except of my weaknesses," he says in verse 5. "I will boast all the more gladly of my weaknesses," he says in verse 9.

What in the world is he talking about? What does it mean to boast in weakness?

I think by "boasting in weakness" Paul means that we ought to own our weakness. To own *up* to it.

It does *not* mean throwing a pity party. It does not mean having a martyr's complex. It does not mean being Debbie Downer. It does not mean the kind of self-conscious self-deprecation that actually brings more attention to one's self. It is not a false humility.

It simply means owning up to the reality that if it were not for Jesus Christ, everything about us would blow apart in the gale-force hurricane of our own sin and frailty.

There is more security, in fact, with Christ in the middle of a stormy sea than without Christ in the warm stillness of our bathtub.

In fact, the end of verse 10 unlocks the purpose of boasting (or *owning*) our weakness: "For when I am weak, then I am strong."

When I had to resign pastoral ministry I felt very vulnerable. My weakness was showing through, and I had to share it (repeatedly) with others looking for an explanation. "God told me," apparently didn't work. And I understand why. But the reasons I supposed God was leading me away didn't seem to make sense to others either. I spoke about my shallow leadership capacity, my inability to see "systems" or keep ahead of the growth of the church. Where everyone else saw success, I was experiencing ever-expanding weakness. They saw all the shiny things floating on the surface of the rising tide, while I felt the waters closing in around my neck and rising up above my nose.

And while I used to think that "doing great things for God" felt like walking on water, I discovered that it very often feels more like drowning.

God was asking me to admit that I could not swim. He was telling me to trust totally in him, not in my own sense of accomplishment and not even in others' positive appraisal of my ministry.

But the weird thing is, in the spiritual economy of the kingdom you find yourself by losing. You live by dying.

See, I had it backward. I thought God was asking me to lay down pastoral ministry and sit down. But really he was telling me to rise up and walk. He was telling me to lay aside all the things I'd been using, the props if you will, to show my strength and simply follow him that he might be *all*. That *he* would be my strength.

"When I am weak, he is strong."

I was called to ministry through a reading of the call of Moses (beginning in Exodus 3). I was in junior high and I was having my morning devotional at a youth camp. There was something about Moses's interaction with the Lord's call that struck me in a very powerful and peculiar way. For one thing, Moses had a ton of excuses. "I'm a nobody; I have no qualifications; I'm a stutterer." (That last one really resonated with me, as I was a stutterer from kindergarten all the way into college.)

And I know what Moses is thinking when he's saying these things. I know what he wants. He wants God to say, "Oh, come on, Moses! You're awesome! That's why I picked you. You're good enough, smart enough, and, doggone it, people like you." At least, that's what I want to hear God say when I'm listing my inadequacies to him.

But God doesn't puff Moses up. He doesn't raise his self-esteem. In fact, he sort of confirms all the disqualifications Moses raises about himself. God says, "I made your tongue. I'll give you my power. *I will be with you.*"

God was not trying to convince Moses that Moses was strong enough for the job. He was telling Moses that God himself was strong enough for the job.

Our weakness is no hindrance to God. In fact, he seems to prefer it! If only because the less of us there is, the more of him shines through, and the more glory he gets.

Don't be afraid of your weakness. It's the only thing God will work with! And the weaker you are, the stronger you will discover your Savior to be. You need not fear.

The Lord's grace is all-sufficient for weakness. It goes all the way down to our need.

Grace Goes All the Way Down to Our Deepest Pain

Grace is all-sufficient for suffering.

In speaking of his weakness, Paul sketches out a curious predicament:

So to keep me from becoming conceited because of the surpassing greatness of the revelations, a thorn was given me in the flesh, a messenger of Satan to harass me, to keep me from becoming conceited. Three times I pleaded with the Lord about this, that it should leave me. But he said to me, "My grace is sufficient for you, for my power is made perfect in weakness." (2 Cor. 12:7–9)

What is this thorn? We don't know. It could be literally physical ailments. (Paul mentions his flesh and refers to weakness.) It could be satanic oppression. (Paul attributes the immediate work to "a messenger of Satan.") It could be both—a satanic oppression that physically torments him. John Calvin seemed to think that Paul is referring to temptations, lures from the devil that attempt to distract him from his mission. Satan wants to derail Paul's ministry.

In any event, whatever this experience is, we know that it's painful—Paul calls it a "thorn . . . in the flesh." It is a constant, nagging pain of some kind, whether physical or psychological or both. And Paul has pleaded with God to take it away. His reference to praying "three times" may refer to literally asking three times or it could signify completion, as in, "I have repeatedly prayed for this to the point of being 'done' praying about it, given the Lord's answer."

I bet you've been there. I bet you've prayed those "I just want this to be over" kind of prayers. Maybe you've faced an illness or medical condition that causes you incredible pain that never goes away and seems like it never will, and you have found yourself pleading with God, over and over again, "Please, Lord, take this pain away from me!" Maybe you've been struggling with depression for a long time, and other people are getting frustrated with you and wonder why you can't just "snap out of it," and you've tried to tell them that you would if you could and that you don't want to feel this way, and you've begged God from the depths of your soul, "Take this darkness off of me!" Maybe you've struggled with some besetting sin, over and over again, and you feel such shame, and you repent but wonder if your repentance is too weak, and you've pleaded with God to take the temptation away because you know it's killing you.

Ever been undone from how *done* you are with suffering?

What's really interesting is that while Paul calls the thorn "a messenger of Satan," it's not clear if it is Satan who has "given" it (v. 7) to him. In fact, he doesn't plead with Satan to leave him alone; he pleads with God.

Why? Because suffering and even satanic attack fall under the sovereignty of the mighty God.

I don't know if this was a Job-like situation—God saying to the devil, "Have you considered my servant Paul?" But in any event, it is helpful to see here how the devil is on a leash and doesn't do anything except what he's allowed to by God.

I mean, given the sovereignty of God over all things, we ought to acknowledge that the Bible doesn't teach that grace goes down only until you get to the point where Satan takes over and starts doing *his* work.

No, it's grace all the way down, even into the deep, dank cellar of affliction.

I have a friend named Richard who died at thirty-two years of age, leaving behind a young family. A brain tumor killed him.

Way too many of you know this, but it is not a pretty thing to watch someone die. We watched Richard waste away, basically, reducing from a tall, strong, healthy, energetic guy down to a thin husk of his former self.

When I met Richard, he'd already been diagnosed and was already fighting the cancer. But I could mark the downgrade of his faculties each time we met. As the cancer crowded out more of his brain, Richard began finding it hard to locate certain words in his mental data bank. I remember once, when we were driving to lunch, he asked me, "Do you know what you're going to say at . . . after?" He wasn't trying to avoid saying the word *funeral*. His mind just couldn't locate it.

And we all watched his smart, funny personality drift gradually away. We watched him fade into the shadows.

Richard was adamant all along about the gospel being preached at his funeral. He knew I wouldn't preach anything else, but it was a point he stressed several times over the last year with me. He had unbelieving family members and friends, and in his mind, if his funeral was what God would use to win the lost, he was all for it.

Eventually he ran out of words. He just couldn't talk. A few weeks before his death I went looking through old emails just to hear his voice, and I found an old message dated September 12, 2012. It began with some nuts and bolts about his treatment schedule, some experimental procedure his family was taking him to Boston for, but he concluded his message in a rather startling way. I don't remember being struck by these lines the first time I read the email, but this time I was eager to recapture some of his personality and his resolve, and the following statement wrecked me:

I really feel so blessed that God would actually use me at all to attempt to bring Him the glory He so deserves. Why me, brother?

Did you catch that? "Why me?" Where many would say, "Why me?" in the pitiful sense of, "Why me? Why is God picking on me? Why did *I* get cancer?" Richard was saying, "Why would God choose little old me for this privilege?"

The day after he died, I was sitting on his family's porch with his father. We were reminiscing and going over plans for the coming days. I was trying to tell him how much Richard had meant to me, how much his faith in God had impressed me and challenged me, and how I couldn't believe how his trust in Jesus seemed to get bigger as his own strength got smaller. His dad said, "You know, he was like that from the very beginning."

He said, "When we were sitting in the hospital waiting on the test results—and we didn't know exactly what they'd be, but they'd already told us to expect bad news, so we knew it wasn't going to be anything good—I looked at him and said, 'No father should bury his son.' And Richard looked at me and said, 'No, Dad, this is a good thing. This is a good thing, because God can use it.'"

What?

How do you get to that point? How do you get to the point of looking at your impending death and thinking, *Well, if this is what God wants, it must be good*?

What Richard had committed to was the glory of Christ, and when he felt the sting of suffering, he learned more of the sweetness of Jesus.

It is true that sometimes God doesn't become our only hope until God becomes our only hope.

Richard had discovered the dispensability of his fallen body. He had discovered the dispensability of his own agendas, his own plans, his own aspirations, his own strength. He knew he wasn't going to get to keep them anyway!

Somewhere along the way, a relative had given Richard a rubber bracelet imprinted with the words *God's Got This*. Over the span of a few weeks, I watched it get looser and looser. And the day before he died, as I visited my unconscious friend on his deathbed, I noticed that bracelet hanging there, loosely, on his skeletal wrist.

GOD'S GOT THIS

I suppose whoever gave it to him meant it in the sense that "God's in control of this situation," or even "God has this cancer in his will." Both of those sentiments are true, of course. But I looked at that little rubber ring, perilously close to falling off his thin hand, and thought, *It means God's got Richard.*

As Paul says in 2 Corinthians 4:16, "though outwardly we are wasting away, yet inwardly we are being renewed day by day" (NIV).

What made the difference for Richard? What made the difference for Paul? The presence of Jesus.

We are gradually becoming swallowed up in Jesus! "Therefore I will boast all the more gladly of my weaknesses, so that the power of Christ may rest upon me" (12:9). The power of Christ! This is what Paul means when he uses the word *grace*, by the way.

Did you know there's no such thing as grace? Grace is Jesus. As Sinclair Ferguson says:

There isn't a thing, a substance, or a "quasi-substance" called "grace." All there is is the person of the Lord Jesus—"Christ clothed in the gospel," as John Calvin loved to put it. Grace is the grace of Jesus. . . . There is no "thing" that Jesus takes from Himself and then, as it were, hands over to me. There is only Jesus Himself.[2]

When you are in the pit of suffering—on the verge of death, even—Jesus isn't up in heaven simply blasting you down below with some ethereal virtues. He's not "sending good thoughts"—or worse, "good vibes"—your way. No, when you are laid low in the dark well of despair, when the whole world seems to be crashing down on you, when your next breath seems sure to be your last, Christ Jesus is down in the void with you, holding you. He keeps your hand between his own. He offers his breast for your weary head. He whispers the words of comfort a whisker's breadth from your ear: "And behold, I am with you *always*" (Matt. 28:20, emphasis added). Grace is all-sufficient for weakness and for suffering because Jesus is all-sufficient.

And thank God that this is not the end of the story. Because grace is all-sufficient for glory too. This is where we turn next, as we wrap up our time together.

Because grace doesn't just go all the way down. It goes all the way up.

10 Lurv Wins

(When You Look Forward to the End)

When the Lord restored
the fortunes of Zion,
we were like those who dream.

Psalm 126:1

My gospel is a handful of crumbs. It does not look like much. But it is more than enough. Some see the crumbs and move on. The plate seems distinctly un-regal; the illusion of this meager offering does not comport with the desires of their belly-god.

Some hear in the call to feast on the words of the Lord a provocation calling them in some way a dog, and they scamper away yelping rather than leaning in, head bowed to be patted.

My gospel is fuller than it appears, more satisfying. A morsel of grace is vastly delicious, greater in taste and sustenance than the biggest buffet at the world's shiniest banquet. My gospel is desert manna, a widow's miracle-cake, Elvish lembas bread.

You must trust me on this.

We get to the front of the Communion line at church, or the plate finally reaches our point in the pew, and we take between our fat thumb and forefinger a tiny thread of spongey bread or flesh-thin wafer or hollow pillow of cracker, and we hear in our ears and hearts, "This is Christ's body broken for you."

Really?

"His blood is poured out for the forgiveness of sins."

We hold, in our calloused paw, a thimbleful of juice.

Okay, don't trust me. Trust *him*.

Trust the *principle*. A little yeast, a little seed. The place of death is the place of life.

There is bigness in the littleness if we will have the eyes to see.

The cross seems foolish to those who are dying. But to those who are alive?

In the 2010 documentary *Cave of Forgotten Dreams*, Werner Herzog investigates the incredible artwork in the Chauvet caverns of South France. In 1994, these cave paintings were discovered by geologists and it was a landmark discovery, rewriting much of what historians and anthropologists believed about ancient man. Dating back twenty thousand years, the paintings are vivid and much more advanced than paleontologists would've expected. For instance, the ancient artists drew multiple legs on their animals to convey the impression of movement.

But the place is fragile. Very few are allowed into the cave to view the paintings. And the deeper one works into the cave, the more astounding the artwork becomes. You can see much of this work in the documentary, as Herzog and his tiny crew are given unprecedented access to the delicate and dark passageways. But in one particular scene, a scientist is explaining that up around a particular corner lies the most beautiful, most exquisite artwork of all. Herzog asks to take the cameras back there to see, to show us. His guide explains that no, they are not allowed. We don't get to see this artwork so tantalizingly promised, so wondrously described.

There is a metaphor there. We are in a cave of sorts. Maybe it is like the cave of Plato's parable, where we see on the walls mere shadows of the fire of reality. Around the corner, we are told, lies the great fire, a blazing beauty so wondrous it will fundamentally change everything we believe, everything we perceive, everything we *are*.

The most incredible thing we could ever see is around the corner, we're told. But we can't go there.

Not yet.

To practice followship of Jesus is to believe the descriptions. It is to believe that around the corner where we cannot yet go is the most wonderful thing we could ever imagine—in fact, it is beyond imagination, beyond what we can conceive. Descriptions cannot do this revelation justice. We hear the rumors of this place, read the travelogues of those precious few who trembled as though dead after spending mere seconds in that sacred space, and though we do not see it, we believe.

By God's grace, we believe.

Jesus says that believing because you see is dime-a-dozen faith. The blessing comes to those who don't see and yet believe (John 20:29).

And if you believe, you will see.

I am speaking, of course, of heaven. But that word *heaven* and all its attendant earthly imagery cannot possibly do it justice.

Joy of Joys and Loveliest of Loves

Have you ever loved someone so much you could not contain the amount of love their very existence provoked in you? Have you ever felt like to know someone was to find access to some deep and hidden spring, some endlessly flowing fountain of out-of-body experientiality? (I am making up words here, and I'm going to keep doing it, so just prepare yourself.)

"Love is too weak a word for what I feel. I *luuurv* you, you know, I *loave* you, I *luff* you, two *f*s, yes I have to *invent*!" So says Alvy Singer to his titular lady friend in the classic film *Annie Hall*. He is so overcome by his feelings for Annie that he finds the word *love* unsuitable. He has to invent words. He *lurvs* her. It's a love bigger than love.

This is how I feel about my wife and kids. *Love* is too weak a word. I have to go into some higher language, an angelic tongue, so to speak (pardon the pun), to convey how my heart feels about them.

Incidentally, this is what I think is happening when people say to babies, "Oh, I could just eat you all up!" It's pretty violent and disgusting if you think about it. I mean, on the plane of literality, eating a baby is about the worst thing you can do. But we aren't being literal. The literal adorableness of babies—of our wives and kids—transports us beyond the literal into an apprehension of otherworldly beauty and the otherworldly affections such beauty is owed. "Eating you all up" is the only image we can think of to convey the delicious joy we feel at a baby's adorableness.

Similarly, I think heaven is way beyond our mental bounds. Heaven is where we finally feel and experience—really, literally, tangibly—the love that is greater than our capacity to love and to even think about love. It's when glory swallows up existence as we know it, and all the beauty and wonder and grandeur and exquisite graces of this awesome created world become somehow *more*, some way deeper and more resonant.

Love wins, sure. But really, *lurv* wins.

It is the vision of Christ's cross and empty tomb that we look back to as the grounds of our assurance and power, and it is the vision of Christ's heavenly throne ahead of us and beyond us that is the ground of our blessed hope. And everywhere we look, we are seeing signposts of this vision in the good design of God, provided we actually follow the signs to the glory they point to and do not terminate on them alone.

A woman is self-conscious about the abundance of freckles on her shoulders and neck, but her husband thinks they are lovely. No, he thinks they're *lurvly*. He finds himself staring at them sometimes when they are lying in bed, and he is discombobulated by those freckles. Some people are embarrassed by their freckles. Others think their freckles are cute. In any event, they're just freckles. But to this husband, they're not just freckles. They are a constellation of tiny suns, a fiery sash about her neck.

There is romance to this. And yet there is also risk.

Because as much as this man is undone by the gift of his wife, he can become endangered by mistaking the gift for the Giver. His wife is not The One.

Husbands are not to regard their wives dispassionately. They must heed the fatherly advice to "let your fountain be blessed, and rejoice in the wife of your youth" (Prov. 5:18). That's good marriage advice. It presupposes that the marriage is not new anymore, that you are years into this covenant experiment but you must still find joy in your spouse; you look beyond them even when looking upon them. And, in fact, the more you get to know someone— sins, flaws, and all—the more you must rejoice. The only way to do this is to see them as a sacred mirror reflecting the very glory of God. My wife is more beautiful to me each day precisely because she is growing in Christ in her followship.

But like the freckle-relishing husband, I waste all this joy over the vision of her loveliness if I don't trace it back to and direct it toward the Giver of all good gifts. If we don't follow the trail of those tiny freckly suns to the Sun of righteousness who placed them on creaturely shoulders even as he hung the blazing suns in a thousand cosmos, we don't love our wives or their Maker with the right kind of love.

Nobody writes about this stuff like the master called Jack:

> I believe . . . that the old stab, the old bittersweet, has come to me as often and as sharply since my conversion as at any time of my life whatever. But I now know that the experience, considered as a state of my own mind, had never had the kind of importance I once gave it. It was valuable only as a pointer to something other and outer. While that other was in doubt, the pointer naturally loomed larger in my thoughts. When we are lost in the woods the sight of the signpost is a great matter. He who first sees it cries, "Look!" The whole party gathers round and stares. But when we have found

the road and are passing signposts every few miles, we shall not stop and stare. They will encourage us and we shall be grateful to the authority that set them up. But we shall not stop and stare, or not much; not on this road, though their pillars are of silver and their lettering of gold. "We would be at Jerusalem."[1]

This is where the bread crumbs go. We have to follow the vast array of earthly joys and loves as if we're following a trail of bread crumbs left behind by the mysterious pilgrims who've gone before us.

The bread crumbs may only last for the day, but there are new ones each day and enough for as many days as we're given to follow them to the heavenly Bread of Life.

And it's in these earthly joys and beauties, rightly seen, that we sometimes get glimpses beyond the veil into the very garden of God.

One pilgrim good with the crumbs was Jonathan Edwards. The man chased the sunbeams of God's radiance like almost nobody else, always pointing us to the source of that radiance as the fulfillment and summation of the little fires we see now only dimly.

> The soul that in this world had only a little spark of divine love in it, in heaven shall be, as it were, turned into a bright and ardent flame, like the sun in its fullest brightness, when it has no spot upon it.[2]

Edwards began his career as a lawyer, and even as a pastor and theologian he had an academic, scholarly tenor to his analysis of God's words and ways. He was systematic. He was logical. He was a delineator. And yet even this serious man could not help but get carried affectionately away in trying to somehow arrest the glory of God with the limited economy of English vocabulary.

He isn't the only one. Even the biblical writers, inspired by the very breath of God, wrestled finitely with their vision of the infinite.

Jesus Is the Point of Heaven

Let's revisit now that strange little episode in Paul's second letter to the Corinthians:

> I know a man in Christ who fourteen years ago was caught up to the third heaven—whether in the body or out of the body I do not know, God knows. And I know that this man was caught up into paradise—whether in the body or out of the body I do not know, God knows—and he heard things that cannot be told, which man may not utter. (2 Cor. 12:2–4)

It is difficult to know exactly what is going on here, if only because Paul finds it difficult to know what is going on here. "Was I in body or in spirit only? Who knows? I really don't want to talk about it."

By "third heaven" it seems clear that he is speaking of the place we often refer to simply as heaven, the place where God is. Beyond the first heaven of sky, beyond the second heaven of space, into the land of divinity.

Despite his use of the third person—"I know a man"—we believe Paul is referring to a personal experience, which seems indicated by his ensuing talk about the thorn being given to him to prevent his boasting in such visions.

Paul seems almost embarrassed to talk about this experience. It so "undid" him that he depersonalizes it. But his mention of this incredible experience seems somewhat precipitated by the alleged visions and Gnostic tendencies of the heretics he's writing against. "Oh, you wanna talk about visions," he appears to be saying, "I've got them too. *But visions aren't the point.* Jesus is the point!"

Which is why, we suppose, he waits fourteen years to say anything about it. And when he finally does, he sort of keeps it at arm's length.

Jesus is the point.

I mean, contrast this three-verse, basically two-sentence description with the multimillion-dollar cottage industry of heavenly visitation books! You know the ones. Little Johnny dies and goes to heaven, where he sees his grandpa and his dead dog Fluffy and he gets to sit on St. Peter's lap and his breath smells like bubblegum. Or whatever. These stupid books stand in stark contrast to the biblical record of heavenly visitations, which seem much rarer and much more . . . well, *traumatic.*

Aside from Paul, we can list on one hand the number of believers in God who went to heaven and lived on earth again to tell about it. We've got Isaiah, Ezekiel, and John. And all four of these chaps are in an outright struggle to know what to think about what they've seen. They feel dead terrified. Isaiah is undone. John falls on his face as though deceased. They can't adequately describe it. They are ransacking their vocabulary, the available imagery. They all get turned inside out.

The truth is that the presence of Jesus is *too wonderful* for us. To be swallowed up into his glory defies all realms of imagination and glory.

And Jesus is the point.

Their direction, their attention is totally hijacked by the glory of the Triune God and by the Lamb who sits on the throne.

Contrast this with the working narratives in so many of our modern heavenly visitation books where Jesus almost seems a peripheral figure, a *feature* of heaven but not the focal point. Jesus is the bonus to heaven in these works.

But Jesus is the point of heaven. Finally seeing him face-to-face is the whole point.

If you could imagine a place of otherworldly delights full of bliss and rest, a place with endless pleasure where all your loved ones are united again in a land flowing with your favorite sights and sounds and even hobbies and occupations, but Jesus were not there, this heaven of yours would be hell.

Jesus is the point.

He is the point of that world just as he is the point of this one. If we do not follow the heavenly signposts of this world to the great face of our Lord Jesus Christ, we will miss out on both the joy of that world and the joys of this one.

I recently took up a brilliant biography of George Whitefield by historian Thomas Kidd.[3] I was already somewhat familiar with Whitefield from my time pastoring in New England, where I dug a little into the region's theological heritage and its towering figures. An Anglican from England, Whitefield was a sort of itinerant preacher in the American colonies in the early 1700s, traveling all over to preach the gospel. Wherever he went, immense crowds would come to hear him preach. People would gather in line days in advance to hear this great man of God proclaim the Word. And Whitefield was a pretty gnarly guy. Very overweight and cross-eyed, beset by several medical conditions that caused him great pain, he was not much to look at. But he had a miraculously booming voice and, apparently, a Spiritual anointing that granted him unprecedented response to his simple gospel preaching.

When Whitefield preached, the crowds went crazy. Some came to heckle him. Some came to assault him. Several attempts were made on his life. But many people were ecstatically moved. He would preach and they would cry out, fall down as though slain in the Spirit, scream, tear their clothes, or otherwise fall sway to some kind of charismatic joy and conviction.

And though he was a dynamic preacher, it wasn't just his preaching that caused such effect. Other pastors would take Whitefield's printed sermons and preach them in their own pulpits and the resulting gospel havoc would be almost the same.

So, as I was reading about this incredible response in Kidd's biography, I thought to myself, *I'm going to get some of these sermons.*

I wanted to see what might happen to me!

I ordered a two-volume collection of Whitefield's sermons and began to dig into them straightaway. I read one sermon, then two. I read a few more. I kept reading.

And . . . well, nothing happened. No screaming, no fainting. I didn't rip my shirt off or anything. They are good sermons. Like the preaching of Charles Spurgeon, Whitefield's exposition is characteristically narrative, imagistic. He doesn't do heady theology. He is faithfully showing Jesus in short texts and preaching to the "common man."

I mean, they're good. But nothing profoundly impressive happened to me.

Until . . .

I came across one particular sermon called "Christ the Best Husband." Now I knew a little bit about this message from Kidd's biography, because he spends a little bit of time recounting the circumstance and consequence of it. See, "Christ the Best Husband" was primarily written for and directed to young women—specifically, to young single women perhaps aspiring to marriage.

And just to paint the picture fully for you, I found myself reading this sermon in the cushy leather chair of a public place that was, as far as I can tell, the most masculine environment I could have possibly been in. Three television screens broadcasting three different ball games, leather and wooden furniture, dead things on the walls! Dudes everywhere talking guy stuff. And I sat there reading the sermon *for the ladies.*

And I began to weep, in front of God and everybody. This is the part that did me in:

> Consider who the Lord Jesus is, whom you are invited to espouse yourselves unto. He is the best husband. There is none comparable to Jesus Christ. Do you desire one that is great? He is of the highest dignity, he is the glory of heaven, the darling of eternity, admired by angels, dreaded by devils and adored by saints. For you to be espoused to so great a king, what honour will you have by this espousal?
>
> Do you desire one that is rich? None is comparable to Christ, the fullness of the earth belongs to him. If you be espoused to Christ, you shall share in his unsearchable riches. You shall receive of his fullness, even grace for grace here and you shall hereafter be admitted to glory and shall live with this Jesus to all eternity.

Do you desire one that is wise? There is none comparable to Christ for wisdom. His knowledge is infinite and his wisdom is correspondent thereto. And if you are espoused to Christ, he will guide and counsel you and make you wise unto salvation.

Do you desire one that is strong, who may defend you against your enemies and all the insults and reproaches of the Pharisees of this generation? There is none that can equal Christ in power, for the Lord Jesus Christ hath all power.

Do you desire one that is good? There is none like unto Christ in this regard; others may have some goodness but it is imperfect. Christ's goodness is complete and perfect, he is full of goodness and in him dwelleth no evil.

Do you desire one that is beautiful? His eyes are most sparkling, his looks and glances of love are ravishing, his smiles are most delightful and refreshing unto the soul. Christ is the most lovely person of all others in the world.

Do you desire one that can love you? None can love you like Christ: His love, my dear sisters, is incomprehensible; his love passeth all other loves: The love of the Lord Jesus is first, without beginning. His love is free without any motive. His love is great without any measure. His love is constant without any change and his love is everlasting.[4]

Oh, everything we look for everywhere else *but* God can only be found *in* God!

Every greatness, every wealth, every wisdom, every power, every goodness, every beauty, and every love we are longing for can only be found in him, and in him we find the apex of all these virtues and more. Even the best of all earthly versions of these virtues are but pale substitutes. Even the most joyous marriage, the most blessed parenthood, the most adorable of babies virtually disappears in the radiance of his most joyous of joys, most blessed of blessedness, most adorable of adorableness as the stars disappear when the sun comes up.

This is the way Paul puts it in his first letter to the Corinthians: "For now we see in a mirror dimly, but then face to face. Now I know in part; then I shall know fully, even as I have been fully known" (1 Cor. 13:12). And then he says, "So now faith, hope, and love abide, these three; but the greatest of these is love" (v. 13).

Why is love greater than faith and hope? Because faith (in what Christ has done) and hope (in what Christ is doing and will do) bring us finally into the loveliest of loves, into the very presence, the very lovely life of the God himself who is love.

Grace is not just sufficient for our weakness and our suffering. It is sufficient for glory. God's grace has ensured us a place in this third heaven, in the very Paradise of God.

> Let not your hearts be troubled. Believe in God; believe also in me. In my Father's house are many rooms. If it were not so, would I have told you that I go to prepare a place for you? And if I go and prepare a place for you, I will come again and will take you to myself, that where I am you may be also. (John 14:1–3)

And just as Paul, having seen it, cannot even describe it, we cannot adequately envision what the fulfillment in glory our everlasting sharing in his glory will be like.

We will get turned inside out, upside down. We will be filled with glory and ushered into the hyper-dimensionality of the very place of God. And the further along we follow, the more the Spirit prepares us for this eventuality. The hope gets stronger and stranger.

In his great little book *Godology*, my friend Christian George writes:

> The deeper I dig into God's attributes, the shallower I find myself. The harder I shovel, the thicker the ground. How can anyone describe the indescribable? How can mortal lips pronounce the unpronounceable? Perhaps if our vocal chords had a thousand octaves or our language, a million syllables. But to perfectly articulate the glory of God requires tongues we don't have, words we can't say, and alphabets we can't know.[5]

And I wonder—I wonder!—if God gave Paul this special peek behind the curtain precisely to prepare him for his particular ministry of weakness and suffering. Not that he would boast in the glory but rather in the weakness and suffering, knowing that this kind of glory is awaiting him.

This is how you boast in your weakness and suffering too. This is how you boast in your sorry little devotional life. This is how you boast in your constant inability to get your act together. No, not by seeing a physical revelation of the heaven that awaits you. But by beholding a vision of the glorious Christ, whose power rests on you if you're a believer.

Paul is not proud of his sin. Nor should we be proud of our struggles and our sluggish Christian life. But we "boast" in this way—by owning up to how great a sinner we are because it is the only way to boast in the greatness of our Savior. Like Paul, we boldly claim to be the chief of sinners because we have the chief of Saviors.

Jesus is the point. He is the very point of the mountain we, daunted, climb—the tippety-top.

He is the summit of all our longing and aspiration and desire.

Catching the Wind

Grace is all-sufficient for glory. Grace doesn't just go all the way down to our weakness and suffering; it goes all the way up to our deliverance, all the way up to the throne of God, where our Savior is seated at the right hand of the Father and where, because we have been raised with him and seated with him in the heavenly places, we also have a place.

The grace that sustains us in our weakness and suffering will deliver us to worlds unspeakable. It is the eternal weight of that glory, in fact, that makes for Paul the suffering of this life "a light momentary affliction" (2 Cor. 4:17).

Jesus Christ left the splendor and glory of his home to come endure the weakness of human flesh and experience the suffering of crucifixion unto death, that we might endure the weakness of human flesh and experience suffering unto death with a vision of joining him forever in the splendor and glory of his home.

His grace is all-sufficient for weakness, for suffering, and for glory.

In Ecclesiastes, as Solomon is looking back on how often he terminated his affections on the crumbs and not on the Bread from which they had fallen, he keeps coming back to one sad image: it is like "striving after wind" (1:14,17; 2:11,17, 26; 4:4, 6, 16; 6:9). It's like chasing the wind, like trying to catch smoke.

In Ecclesiastes, all the beauty and meaning Solomon sought in the world only satisfied for a moment and then it was gone, *poof*, like a vaporous nothing. He calls it "vanity" and "meaningless." The whole tapestry of the world he is weaving becomes unraveled at the end of every line.

In heaven, though, Ecclesiastes is reversed. The tapestry quickly assembles, line by line in quick succession, and the backside of loose threads and disjointed patterns we have struggled to comprehend all our miserable life turns away from us and we see the front side, the full portrait of all God has been doing to renew the world and *us for it*.

In heaven, believe it or not, we will catch the wind!

C. S. Lewis says, "The sweetest thing of all my life has been the longing . . . to find the place where all the beauty came from."[6]

Brothers and sisters, we are going to that place. (Indeed, as we've hopefully already seen, in a very real way, we are already there by our mystical union to Christ.) Behold in your most inside of insides the vision of this place where you can hold the wind in your hands precisely because you are friends with the One who controls it with his very word.

As Jonathan Edwards writes,

> And thus they will love, and reign in love, and in that god-like joy that is its blessed fruit, such as eye hath not seen, nor ear heard, nor hath ever entered into the heart of man in this world to conceive; and thus in the full sunlight of the throne, enraptured with joys that are forever increasing, and yet forever full, they shall live and reign with God and Christ forever and ever![7]

We were built for this. Not just for love, but for the Love all-excelling. We were built for *lurv*. And when we surrender to Christ, we are destined for the day lurv wins.

When we are destined for the day lurv wins—thank God!—we surrender to Christ.

I know it's hard to trust that the best bread is under the table. We have to put ourselves at so many feet, in such dim light, scraping with our shaking hands any crummy morsel that is there. But in the meantime it will do. It will be more than enough. You'll find it a feast if you'll but trust and taste.

Faith is most needed there, down on the floor under that table. But take heart. One day, the Lord will put out his hand and pull us up. What was down will be up. Everything will be set back to rights. He will pull out a chair and seat us at his own table at the wedding supper of the Lamb.

Somehow, every last dumb one of us will get to sit right next to him, and he himself—Christ the best husband—will put his arm around us, and all will be well.

This Conclusion Isn't Very Long

(When You're Almost Done Reading This Book)

What I'm trying to say is this: you are not your quiet time.

Okay, day to day, you kind of *are* your Bible reading. The spiritual disciplines—the rhythms of the kingdom—do shape us and help us become more of what Jesus is making us through them. But in the end, you are not your quiet time.

You are not your cruddy prayer life. Prayer is vital and necessary. When you pray, you strip your soul down to your proper proportion, helpless and needy and desperate. Prayer of all kinds is basically confessed need of God. It is an expression of our un-God-ness and God's total God-ness. But in the end, you are not your prayers. Jesus is mediating for you and the Spirit is interceding for you, making up for all your prayerlessness.

You are not your standing before people.

You are not your past.

You are not the accumulation of harsh words from others and negative self-talk.

You are not even your sin, as primary and as serious as that problem is.

I'm not trying to affirm your sense of goodness. I'm doing the opposite, in fact.

I want to, by God's grace, give you the freedom to own up to your not having your act together. I wrote this book for all who are tired of being tired. I wrote this book for all who read the typical discipleship manuals and wonder who they could possibly be written for, the ones that make us feel overly burdened and overly tasked and, because of all that, overly *shamed*.

You are not your ability to pull yourself up by your own bootstraps.

You are not the sum of your spiritual accomplishments and religious devotion.

You are a great sinner, yes. But you have a great Savior.

Child of God, you are a child of God. And he will never, ever, ever leave you or forsake you.

(See, I told you it wasn't long.)

Notes

Chapter 1 Sin and the Art of Soul Maintenance

1. John Newton, "Twenty-One Letters to Mr. and Mrs. W****," *The Works of John Newton*, vol. 4 (New Haven: Nathan Whiting, 1824), 291.

2. See Psalm 42:5, 11.

Chapter 2 Good News for Losers

1. Ta-Nehisi Coates, *Between the World and Me* (New York: Spiegel and Grau, 2015), 28.

2. Ibid., 29.

3. Ray Ortlund, "Adorned," *Christ Is Deeper Still*, April 9, 2008, http://blogs .thegospelcoalition.org/rayortlund/2008/04/09/adorned/.

Chapter 3 Staring at the Glory until You See It

1. Bob Dylan, "I Shall Be Released," 1967.

2. C. S. Lewis, "On Science Fiction," *"On Stories" and Other Essays on Literature* (San Francisco: Harcourt Brace Jovanovich, 1982), 62.

3. John Piper, "Do You See the Joy of God in the Sun? Part 2," sermon preached at Bethlehem Baptist Church, Minneapolis, Minnesota, August 26, 1990, *Desiring God*, http://www.desiringgod.org/messages/do-you-see-the-joy-of-god-in -the-sun-part-2.

4. G. K. Beale, *We Become What We Worship: A Biblical Theology of Idolatry* (Downers Grove, IL: InterVarsity, 2008), 16.

5. Jonathan Edwards, "The Distinguishing Marks of a Work of the Spirit of God," *The Works of Jonathan Edwards*, vol. 2 (London: Ball, Arnold, and Company, 1840), 257.

6. Charles Spurgeon, *The Autobiography of Charles H. Spurgeon: 1834–1854*, vol. 1 (Cincinnati: Curts and Jennings, 1898), 105.

7. Ibid., 106.

Chapter 4 The Rhythm of Listening

1. George Herbert, "The Holy Scriptures I," *The Temple: Sacred Poems and Private Ejaculations* (Cambridge: Thomas Buck and Roger Daniel, 1633).

2. Dallas Willard, *The Great Omission: Reclaiming Jesus's Essential Teachings on Discipleship* (New York: HarperCollins, 2006), 166. Emphasis in original.

3. Martin Luther, *What Luther Says*, vol. 1, ed. Ewald M. Plass (St. Louis: Concordia, 1959), 67.

4. Herbert, "Holy Scriptures I."

5. "What *Reveal* Reveals," *Christianity Today* 52, no. 3 (March 2008), 27, http://www.christianitytoday.com/ct/2008/march/11.27.html.

6. "Survey Shows the Transformative Impact of Bible Reading & Reflection on Churches," Scripture Union online, accessed October 5, 2016, http://www.scriptureunion.org/SU%20resources/WillowCreekSurvey-RP.pdf.

Chapter 5 The Rhythm of Spilling Your Guts

1. John Ortberg, *The Life You've Always Wanted* (Grand Rapids: Zondervan, 1997), 82.

2. Mark Henderson, "Media Multitaskers Are in Danger of Brain Overload," *Times*, August 25, 2009, http://www.thetimes.co.uk/tto/technology/article1967439.ece.

Chapter 6 The Revolution Will Not Be Instagrammed

1. John Wesley, *The Letters of John Wesley*, ed. George Eayrs (London: Hodder and Stoughton, 1915), 19.

2. Dietrich Bonhoeffer, *Life Together: A Discussion of Christian Fellowship* (San Francisco: Harper & Row, 1954), 23.

3. Skye Jethani, *The Divine Commodity* (Grand Rapids: Zondervan, 2009), 143.

4. See Larry Osborne, *Sticky Church* (Grand Rapids: Zondervan, 2008), 140–41. Also Scott Boren, "Why Small Groups Don't Work in America," *ChurchLeaders*, accessed September 23, 2016, http://www.churchleaders.com/smallgroups/small-group-articles/153896-why-small-groups-don-t-work-in-america.html.

5. Tim Chester and Steve Timmis, *Total Church: A Radical Reshaping around Gospel and Community* (Wheaton: Crossway, 2008), 45.

6. Bonhoeffer, *Life Together*, 30–31.

7. Jared C. Wilson, *The Pastor's Justification: Applying the Work of Christ in Your Life and Ministry* (Wheaton: Crossway, 2013).

8. Bonhoeffer, *Life Together*, 78.

Chapter 7 The Nine Irrefutable Laws of Followship

1. Dallas Willard, *The Divine Conspiracy: Rediscovering Our Hidden Life in God* (San Francisco: HarperCollins, 1998), 142. Emphasis in original.

2. Brant Hansen, "More Excerpts from 'The 417 Rules of Awesomely Bold Leadership': The Enemy of Awesomely Awesome is Pretty Awesome," *Letters from Kamp Krusty*, January 2008, http://branthansen.typepad.com/letters_from _kamp_krusty/2008/01/more-excerpts-f.html.

3. Jared C. Wilson, *Knowing the Bible: Romans* (Wheaton: Crossway, 2014), 23.

4. Richard Sibbes, *The Bruised Reed and Smoking Flax* (London: Pickering, 1838), 30.

Chapter 8 Will the Real Me Please Stand Up?

1. Søren Kierkegaard, *Søren Kierkegaard's Journals and Papers: Autobiographical Part One, 1829–1848*, vol. 5, ed. and trans. Howard V. Hong and Edna H. Hong (Bloomington: Indiana University Press, 1978), 443.

2. Charles Spurgeon, "A Bottle in the Smoke," sermon preached March 23 1856, in *The Complete Sermons of C.H. Spurgeon*, book 1, ed. David Attebury (Attebury: Louisville, 2015), 208.

3. Martin Luther, *Letters of Spiritual Counsel*, trans. and ed. Theodore G. Tappert (Vancouver: Regent College, 2003), 86–87.

4. Mike Hawkins, "November 18, 2015: Chapel with Dr. Mike Hawkins," Vimeo video, 34:51, posted by Midwest Baptist Theological Seminary, November 18, 2015, https://vimeo.com/146157054.

5. Martin Luther, "A Mighty Fortress Is Our God," 1529.

Chapter 9 Does Grace Go All the Way Down?

1. John Rippon, "How Firm a Foundation," 1787.

2. Nathan W. Bingham, "By Grace Alone: An Interview with Sinclair Ferguson," Ligonier Ministries, June 6, 2014, http://www.ligonier.org/blog/grace -alone-interview-sinclair-ferguson/.

Chapter 10 Lurv Wins

1. C. S. Lewis, *Surprised by Joy* (New York: Harcourt, Grace & World, 1955), 238.

2. Jonathan Edwards, *Heaven: A World of Love* (Lindenhurst, NY: Great Christian Books, 2010), 26.

3. Thomas S. Kidd, *George Whitefield: America's Spiritual Founding Father* (New Haven: Yale University Press, 2014).

4. George Whitefield, *The Sermons of George Whitefield*, vol. 1, ed. Lee Gatiss (Wheaton: Crossway, 2012), 117–18.

5. Christian George, *Godology* (Chicago: Moody, 2009), 160.

6. C. S. Lewis, *Till We Have Faces: A Myth Retold* (New York: Harcourt, 1956), 75.

7. Edwards, *Heaven*, 47.

Jared C. Wilson is Director of Content Strategy for Midwestern Baptist Theological Seminary in Kansas City, Missouri, and managing editor of For the Church (ftc.co). He is the author of numerous books, including *Unparalleled*, *The Story of Everything*, *The Prodigal Church*, and *Gospel Wakefulness*. His writing has appeared in *Tabletalk*, *Rev!* magazine, Exponential's *Leadership Learnings*, *Pulpit Helps* magazine, and numerous other publications. His blog, *The Gospel-Driven Church*, is hosted by the Gospel Coalition, and he speaks at numerous churches and conferences throughout the year. Wilson lives near Kansas City.

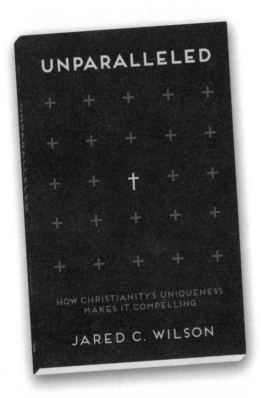